Aman,
Always Remember,
"It's Great to Be You!"

Roy Lane

It's Great to Be YOU!

NOW, more than ever, you must realize the power of YOU.

Raymond A. Saint

POSITIVE FOCUS, INC.

IT'S GREAT TO BE YOU!
NOW, MORE THAN EVER, YOU MUST REALIZE
THE POWER OF YOU.

Available at www.raysaint.com

© 2009 by Raymond A. Saint

All rights reserved. No part of this book may be reproduced or transmitted in any form or by any means, electronic or mechanical, including photocopying, recording, or by any information storage and retrieval system, without permission in writing from the publisher.

Published by Positive Focus Incorporated

P.O. Box 83

Boscobel, WI 53805

Limit of Liability/Disclaimer of Warranty: While the publisher and author have used their best efforts in preparing this book, they make no representations or warranties with respect to the accuracy or completeness of the contents of this book and specifically disclaim any implied warranties of merchantability or fitness for a particular purpose. The advice and strategies contained herein may not be suitable for your situation. Neither the publisher nor the author shall be liable for any loss of profit or any other commercial damages, including, but not limited to, special, incidental, consequential, or other damages.

ISBN: 978-0-9823247-0-7 (Hardcover)

Illustrator: Dirk Boelman
www.dirkboelman.com

Printed in the United States of America

TOOLBOX
(TABLE OF CONTENTS)

ABOUT THE AUTHOR	vii
ACKNOWLEDGEMENTS	ix
AUTHOR'S MESSAGE	xi
THE BEGINNING	15
GET-IT TOGETHER	23
THE "I" IN TEAM	29
ATTITUDE	39
GOALS	47
COMMITMENT	57
STANDARD OF EXCELLENCE	61
FOCUS & SELF-DISCIPLINE	67
SUCCESS	75
SUCCESS TRIANGLE	81
STRESS	91
PRODUCTIVITY	99
DECISION-MAKING PROCESS	107

IT DOESN'T MATTER	113
PRIORITIES	117
FEAR OF FAILURE	123
LEADERSHIP	129
COMMUNICATION	137
INTENT	145
5 SYSTEMS OF THE BODY	151
INSPIRATION	161
WHAT'S RIGHT?	169
LIFESTYLE CHANGE	175

About the Author

Ray Saint has been building leaders and teaching others to be successful on purpose for most of his adult life. He has led by example and speaks from experience. As a Certified Protection Specialist and a graduate at the top of his class from ESI, Executive Security International, in 1989, Ray has first hand knowledge and hands on experience in areas including profiles of terrorism, observational psychology, combat and defensive shooting, executive protocol, personal protection, hand to hand combat, and escape and evasive driving tactics. He has provided personal protective services to World Leaders and corporate executives throughout North America. These experiences have given Ray a unique approach to personal growth, goal setting, and developing strategies for his own success. They have enabled him, through his own desires, motivation, and goal setting to better inspire others to reach and fulfill their dreams and goals. Ray is also a Master Instructor (5th degree black belt) and has twenty-six years experience in the martial arts disciplines of Tae Kwon Do and Hap Ki Do. Over this period of time, he has taught over ten thousand individuals the positive leadership traits of self-maximization.

Ray, through his company, Positive Focus Inc., has been providing Personal Development and Leadership Training to organizations and individuals for the past fifteen years. He provides his clients with "real-time" solutions and practical applications that are guaranteed to affect the bottom line both personally and professionally. His unique ability to inspire individuals, from the front line to the boardroom, has made him a sought after inspirational leader. His keynotes, workshops, and seminars are built around the unique needs of his clients and are nationally recognized as being thought provoking, humorous, and educational.

As a Director of Safety and Employee Development in a corporate setting, Ray has developed and implemented unique training programs for maximizing potential in companies employing from five hundred to six thousand employees.

As a personal success and life balance coach, Ray has coached executive and management level individuals in getting re-focused and re-energized towards a balanced approach to success and happiness in their lives.

As a professional speaker and published author, Ray will re-energize you, your company, organization, or association. Through the use of the tools in this book, Ray will guide you to develop a greater understanding of your role as the "I" in team, to encourage and enable you to incorporate success in your life, at home, at work, or at play.

Acknowledgements

There are far too many people to acknowledge and, to give credit to for this book becoming a reality. What gives me comfort is the fact that I know that you know who you are and what impact you have had on my life as a friend, peer, mentor, co-worker, acquaintance, stranger, or enemy; you have had an effect on this book's content.

The people whom I need to acknowledge by name are those immediately responsible for the task of getting me to put it on the paper, which you are reading now. Dorothy Miller is a wonderful woman whom I had known, but never really met until I spoke to a cancer support group to which she and my mother, as cancer survivors, had belonged. During my presentation, I mentioned to the group that I was writing a book, although it was only in my head at the time. Dorothy, soon after, sent me a letter thanking me for the presentation and said, "You must get that book done, as soon as possible." She wanted to have the first copy. Dorothy felt my material was inspiring to people and she felt that it could benefit people whether they were battling disease, life issues, or other struggles. For nine plus years, I have carried those kind words with me, and if not for Dorothy, this book would have stayed in my head. Dorothy, with great respect for your patience and perseverance, the first copy is yours.

Secondly, getting this book from my head to paper was not an easy task. I am a speaker, instructor, life coach, and trainer, not a writer. Enter Delores Faulkner, a true editorial blessing. I had seen a letter to the editor in our local newspaper that she had written, and I thought it was a beautifully crafted letter that pulled me along. Turns out, she was an accomplished writer. What are the odds of finding a published author in a small rural community who lives five blocks from me and who is willing to take on the daunting task of editing this project? Little did I know that Delores was to become the editor in chief (boss), junior editor, and any other editor necessary to bring this book to fruition. Her ability to take my "speaker's talk" and wordsmith it into this readable piece of work truly amazed and inspired me chapter after chapter. Delores, your excitement and belief in this project kept it moving forward and, sometimes to your dismay, growing! Your wonderful talent of understanding the passion and intent of my thoughts, ideas, and words has been invaluable to this project. It would not have happened if not for you, boss! Thank you.

Lastly, I must thank Ms. Jean Salzgeber, proofreader extraordinaire. Your passion for and command of the English language is inspiring. The book will be an enjoyable and beneficial read for many people thanks to your diligence with grammar, punctuation, and structure. Your expertise has been invaluable, and I thank you for sharing it with this project.

Author's Message

The key to getting the most out of this book is knowing right up front that It's Great to Be You. Fortunately, for you, I did not fill it with guaranteed formulas for success or give you ten key steps to lead you. It does not come with a secret potion or a bag of goods as others may try to sell you. The good news for you is that this book is your toolbox; it is as individual as you are, and it is filled with necessary tools, which have been around for thousands of years. These are the tools that you need to be successful on purpose. I know, I just told you that I was not going to "give you anything."

Let me clarify the intent of this book. The sole intent is to share with you proven tools that leaders and successful people have been using for years. When I talk about leaders and successful people, I am talking about people just like you and me. We are all the same, each trying our best, day-by-day, to make it through this life. Not one of us is better than the next; we just have different roles. Some are living the life that they want, and others are not.

When I say leaders and successful people "just like you and me," I am talking about the single mother who is raising a child or children because she wants to. She realizes that she needs to plan, schedule, and problem solve, using leadership skills daily. I am talking about the factory worker who is happy producing a product for others and giving his best to the company. His attitude is that he doesn't "have" to go to work each day, he "gets" to go to work. I am talking about the owner of her small company who devotes fourteen hours each day to assure its success and loves it. Doing what you want to be doing is being successful.

I believe that the tools in this book are proven to be necessary if you want to be successful on purpose; however, you must find your own truths in these tools and how they apply to you in your life. No one, including me, can do that for you. The beauty of it, as you'll soon discover, is that the tools will work for you individually. How and in what way will you apply these tools to assure success through your life journey?

Benjamin Franklin said, "Life is meant to be enjoyed, everything else is but a mockery." I hope that you can apply the tools shown in this book to maximize your potential, but most of all, I hope that you enjoy the journey!

"We do not choose to be born. We do not choose our parents, the country of our birth or the immediate circumstances of our upbringing. We do not, most of us, choose to die; nor do we choose the time or conditions of our death. But within all this choicelessness, we do choose how we shall live our lives."

Joseph Epstein

*This book is dedicated to
Mr. Larry Leitzinger and Dr. Brent Kooistra
who are two of the truest leaders on this planet.*

THE BEGINNING...

THE BEGINNING…

The content of this book might ruffle some feathers and go against many ideas that you may have been taught. Your parents, teachers, or even your high school coaches may have told you, "There is no "I" in team!" I am telling you there is an "I" in team, and the "I" is YOU.

This book began as a dream; however, with the use of several tools, which you will learn about within its chapters, I have made it a reality. It's Great to Be You is already a resounding success! I know this because I have been living the simple concepts and using the tools in this book for the last five years, and my quality of life has improved personally as well as professionally. I now control my life. Have you ever found yourself asking the following questions? "How can I get more control of my life?" "Why do these things happen to me?" "Why can't I be as lucky as she is?" If you have, then I believe this book is for you.

I have purposely kept this book in the form of a practical guide because I believe that life itself is simple; it is just not easy. "We" complicate our life through many of our own actions. In order to receive the benefits from the simple truths contained in this book, you must first grasp and embrace this concept: "Your life WILL become easier once you have an understanding of just how much of it YOU actually control."

You already know your life is very busy, so busy, in fact, that you do not have the time to learn a whole new vocabulary or complex formulas that self-proclaimed "happiness gurus" say you need in order to be successful. Not only do you not have time for it, but also you do not need it. I believe that we can all be successful no matter what our lot in life as long as we view the world from the inside out and GET-IT Together in our individual lives.

You will find the GET-IT Together philosophy in this book is opposite from others that you may have read; in that, we must simplify and not complicate the process. The GET-IT Together philosophy applies practical concepts or tools of which you are probably already aware. The goal is to use the right tool at the right time to get the desired result. For example, I could have the very best ¾ inch wrench ever made, but if I am trying to loosen a ½ inch nut, it is a useless tool for the job.

In this book, we will discuss the practical tools and their benefit to you, as you work towards reaching your goals.

Look around you in your everyday life, and you'll see people just wandering through life with no direction as if they are a pinball being hit around at random or a beach ball in the water on a windy day. I have often wondered why people function in this manner as if they had no real desire to excel or create a good life for themselves. They allow themselves to be pushed about or blown around without ever trying to set their own course and implement the tools necessary to navigate through their desired destination.

We are all familiar with the negative person that tears one down or feels the world has a vendetta against him/her, always finding and pointing out the bad in everyone and everything. I find it interesting to watch and listen to those who believe that, no matter what they do, the world will make it go wrong, and it won't be through any fault of their own. The reality is that they may not want to be this way and that they just don't know how to change it. Perhaps from the time they were old enough to comprehend, they were told "no" and "don't" so many times that they just gave up and stopped trying to express themselves. Feeling good about our life and ourselves is something we all desire, yet few of us ever attain. If you are one of these people, if it is something you really want, you can change and be whoever you choose to be, and that, my friend, is the not so "secret" secret.

It is my hope that by the time you finish reading this book, you will have a much keener understanding of how you truly do control many of the events that happen in life, to you, for you, and because of you. There are those who want things to happen, those who let things happen, and those who make things happen. Which will you be? The choice is up to you!

Instead of asking "Why does everyone else have all the luck?" or "Why is he/she the one instead of me?" you should be asking, "Who am I, Where am I going, What do I want?" "If I don't have it, how do I plan to get it?" These are the questions you must first ask and answer for yourself. Once you have honestly asked and answered these four "simple" questions, your life will change forever, and you will be on the road towards personal and professional success and truly GET-IT Together.

This book is meant to be a practical guide and everything in it will not pertain to everyone all of the time. If, at times, it appears as though I am talking directly to you, and you sense that what I'm saying is just for you, it is possible that it is relevant to you at this point and time in your life, and you should pay particular attention.

The sad news is that only about five percent of the people reading this book now will take the necessary steps towards implementing the personal goals and strategies into their lives to make a real difference.

The good news is that if you are part of that five percent, you will understand the opportunities available to you are in direct relation to your commitment to YOU, and once you grasp that, it should excite and energize YOU beyond imagination.

Please note that the chapters in this book are not in any particular order of importance because that may be determined by what your goals are for your life and where you currently are towards reaching those goals. The chapters in this book are what I call tools, or building blocks, that are necessary for being successful "on purpose."

As a practical guide, you should refer to this book when your life is going well, when it is not going well, and when you want to purposely make a change in your life. This book is now yours. Highlight areas, make notes, and add your thoughts, contemplations, and successes to these pages. My hope is that you refer to them often as you reach your goals and plan new ones.

My reason for bringing this practical tool to you is that you will realize that "it's great to be you" and the "I" in team is YOU. You will use this as a guide towards meeting and exceeding the personal and professional expectations that YOU set for yourself throughout your life.

Toolbox Takeaway:
You should refer to this book when your life is going well, when it is not going well, and when you purposely want to make a change in your life.

Below, write your answers to the questions; Who am I, Where am I going, What do I want, How do I plan to get it?

_____

_____

_____

_____

_____

_____

_____

_____

_____

_____

_____

It's Great to Be You!

GET-IT TOGETHER

"Life is simple; it just isn't easy."

R. Saint

GET–IT TOGETHER

Earlier, I told you the GET-IT Together concept is one of simplicity, not complexity. Because our lives today are so busy and complicated, most of us could benefit by simplifying them. In order to be happy and successful in our lives, we all need to GET-IT Together.

The GET-IT acronym stands for the following:

G= Goals
E= Energy/emotion
T= Technique

I= Inner skills
T= Testing

Let's go over the acronym briefly; I will discuss it in greater depth throughout the remaining chapters in the book.

G = Goal. If you want to be successful or happy on purpose, you must always have a goal. Your goal may be simple. You may want no more than to wake up each day and inhale and exhale (which, by the way, is a good goal to have); fortunately, for most of us, this is already being controlled by our respiratory system, so we do not have to spend a lot of our day thinking about that process! In a later chapter, I'll discuss the four remaining essential systems of our body.

E = Energy/emotion. For every goal to become reality, you must put energy and/or emotion into it. This is the fuel necessary to move your goal(s) forward.

T = Technique. Using the right communication technique is vital in every situation if you want to reach your goal.

I = Inner skills. Every situation in life should enhance your inner skills. Each one, good or bad, should be viewed as a learning tool to keep you from repeating the same mistakes over and over again, thereby allowing you to grow.

T = Testing. You should use the GET-IT Together concept as a guide in testing yourself every day as you work through the following checkpoints:

Do I have a goal?
Am I putting the right energy and emotion into it?
Am I using the proper technique/communication in each situation?
Am I enhancing my inner skills?
Am I constantly testing myself as each new situation arises so that I can continue to be where I should be and GET-IT Together in my life?

This should simplify the GET-IT concept for you:

If you have a clear **GOAL**, you can direct your **ENERGY** through the **TECHNIQUE** that best fits the situation to achieve your goal. You should use all situations to develop your **INNER SKILLS,** and you should **TEST** everything. Assume responsibility for what you create through your words, thoughts and actions.

The most important part of the preceding paragraph is that you must assume responsibility for what you create with your words, thoughts, and actions. This will eliminate all opportunity for placing blame, which I personally believe is one of the most useless words in the English language. Allow me to explain.

If you believe that you are responsible for your words, thoughts, and actions and that only you are responsible for what is created through them, then you know that blame is useless. No one ever benefits from blame. Blaming serves two purposes only; first, it hurts one of the parties involved, and second, it wastes the time and energy of the other. It robs both parties by consuming their thoughts and resources, and it delays their time in reaching their goals.

In his 9 rules of strategy, Miyamoto Musashi, Japan's greatest samurai, said, "Do nothing which is of no use." Having negative attitudes, blaming others, and hurting others are all thoughts and actions that are of no use.

GET-IT Together is a great tool to help keep you focused on your goals and potential successes.

Toolbox takeaway:

Placing blame robs both parties by consuming their thoughts and resources and delaying their time in reaching their goals.

Below, list what you need to do to simplify your life?

_____

_____

_____

_____

_____

_____

_____

_____

_____

_____

It's Great to Be You!

THE "I" IN TEAM

"You are your greatest asset; it is great to be you."

R. Saint

It's Great to Be You!

THE "I" IN TEAM

The philosophy of the "I" in team is as simple as understanding that YOU are your own greatest asset. Your greatest asset is not the new car that you bought, care for, keep clean, and maintain well. Your greatest asset is not your house that you worked many years to obtain. Your greatest asset is not your bank account, which you work hard to build and make grow. As your greatest asset, you must understand that you need to take time to love and nurture yourself first by knowing who you are, what you want, and if you don't have it, how you're going to get it. You must commit yourself to this if you want to maximize your potential. Think about it; if you did not have you, what would you have? The answer is nothing. It only stands to reason that you must focus on you, the "I" in team.

Example: I often think of the NBA basketball team, the Chicago Bulls. As a native to the Chicago area, I have always been a Bulls fan. When Michael Jordan came to the Bulls, it definitely made for an exciting team. Michael Jordan, to this day, is arguably the best basketball player to ever play the game. However, even though Michael could manage to score fifty plus points a game, the Bulls, as a team, were still not maximizing their full potential. I remember the game when Michael scored sixty-three points against the Celtics, and the Bulls still lost. Why? The rest of the players were not able to maximize their individual potential and be the "I" in team. Once the players figured out that there were five people on the floor, instead of one person, they began to win. The Bulls went on to win six championships in ten years, with championships three years in a row, twice! This is the value of people understanding the "I" in team. Successful teams are made up of individuals who know who they are, what they want, and how they get it. Working together, each as their own "I" in team, they were able to maximize the potential of the entire team. Phil Jackson, the Bulls' head coach at the time, once said, "The success of the individual is in the team, and the success of the team is in the individual."

When talking about the success of individuals, it is important to note that every self help or rehabilitation program addressing issues such as abuse or drugs and alcohol, has at its core, the belief in self. Again, you are the "I" in team.

I have personally known drug addicts and alcoholics who never came to the realization that they were the "I" in team. Why would you take your greatest asset, YOU, and purposely try to harm it? Why would you take cigarettes, knowing that tobacco has sixty-nine known cancer causing properties, and purposely put that smoke in the life-giving lungs of your greatest asset? Why? You do not understand your own personal value. For example, would you take your brand new car and pour a bucket of hot tar all over it? I don't think you would, but you will smoke cigarettes and pour that tar into your lungs. If you don't think your lungs are important, try closing your mouth and pinching your nose. You will be out of this world in less than three minutes. (I don't suggest trying this at home!) You should now understand the importance of your lungs. Try living without your liver. It is impossible, yet you think nothing of killing it off a little at a time by making it process the alcohol that you run through it on a frequent basis. I am not trying to judge you or tell you what you should or shouldn't do. I am just stating proven facts that are known to have negative, if not deadly, effects on the human mind and body. As with everything else in your life, you choose your words, thoughts, and actions. Choose wisely.

One reason so many people do not realize that they are the "I" in team is because they have been brought up that way. When we were little, our parents taught us to be nice to our neighbor or to help the elderly person by holding the door for him/her. Though these are very important values to teach our children, how many parents actually sit their kids down and say, "Honey, I would like you to take five hours a week just for yourself and for your physical and emotional development, okay?"

When I give keynotes, workshops, and seminars, I often ask people to look around the room and pick out anyone whom they believe has the ability to be successful or reach a goal that would help them be happier in life. I then ask them to share their answer with the group. I would say that 99.9% of the time, no one picks himself. Why? People have been trained to think of themselves last.

We have been conditioned, and continue to condition our children, to pay attention to everyone else before ourselves. I disagree with this thought process. I spoke to a group of parents at a technical college a few years ago, and after talking about this concept, one parent later approached me to tell me that he felt he owed his son an apology for raising him to care about everyone else more than himself. In the Bible, it says that we should love our neighbor as we love ourselves. It does not say that we are to love others and (then) ourselves, or others (more) than ourselves, but (as) ourselves. You need to love and nurture yourself and take the time to know who you are and for what you stand if you truly want to love your neighbor as yourself. If we first love our self totally and completely, then the love that we extend to our neighbor will be of the highest quality. You need to take at least five hours a week just for YOU, without your spouse, friends, or pets. Just you! You need to do this so that you can remind yourself of who you are, where you're going, what you want, and if you don't have it, how you are going to get it. Stay focused, and reaffirm your goals to yourself every day. I say this to you, as the "I" in team, you must love, care for, and nurture yourself before you can truly move forward and give 100% to those in your life for whom you say you love and care.

You do not get more out of life than you put into it. The "I" in team is by no means being conceited, uncaring, or arrogant. It is simply knowing that you must give to yourself in order to be the person you want to be and deserve to be. Only then can you truly give to others with pure, loving intent.

The most destructive element to the human being is to not reach your true, full potential, whatever that is. We are all created for a purpose; each is to take from life and to give back to life. Striving to reach your true potential can involve risk, chance, and discomfort. Many people fail to follow their hearts and minds because of the fear of these elements. While this scares some, it excites and invigorates others.

If you are happy with where you are in your life and career, and you are doing what you want to be doing, then congratulations! You are successful on purpose and should be continually striving to maximize your potential. However, if you desire more than where you are, if you want to be self-employed, if you desire to move up in the organization, or if you have a great idea for a career, then you must develop a goal and strategy to make this happen for you. If you don't, eventually this will erode your self-confidence and self-worth, making you unhappy and unfulfilled personally, as well as professionally. Should of, could of, would of, and didn't will prevent you from pushing forward to create a better life for yourself and will constantly weigh you down by reminding you of your past mistakes and failures.

You know who and what you are. You are both happy and fulfilled, or you are not. As the "I" in team, you must control what you can control, not try to control what you can't. This is the only way to maximize your potential both personally and professionally. You owe it to yourself.

Every day when you wake up, say this to yourself:
I am my greatest asset….
Today I will…

Be productive.
Make good choices.
Pursue my goals.

If you can say this to yourself every day, you will be working towards maximizing your potential as the "I" in team. Will you be productive, make good choices, and pursue your goals every day? Probably not. However, if you say this to yourself every day, you will be purposely working towards your eventual success.

Toolbox takeaway:

Successful teams are made up of individuals who know who they are, what they want, and how they get it.

Below, write a note to yourself explaining who you are and why you are your greatest asset.

_____

_____

_____

_____

_____

_____

_____

_____

_____

The "I" in Team

It's Great to Be You!

ATTITUDE

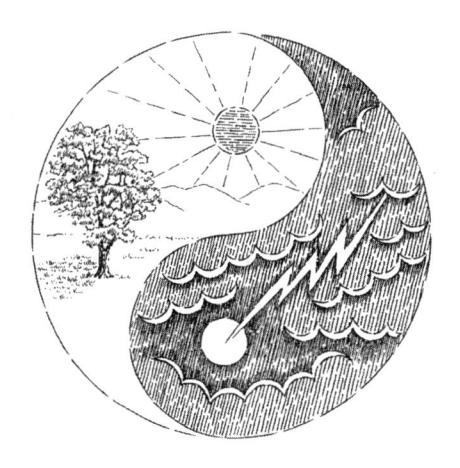

"You are what you're thinking all day long."

R. W. Emerson

ATTITUDE

Let's talk about your attitude. There are no gray areas in attitude. Your attitude each day will be good, or your attitude will be bad, - it's black or white. No one else can or should be allowed to choose your attitude for you. You have 100% control, and when you remember that YOU are the "I" in team, you will take control of your thoughts and emotions. You will choose to be positive regardless of the negative people and negative attitudes around you.

You may believe that because your boss was short and rude with you, she gave you a bad attitude, or it was something your friend or family member said that put you in a bad mood. The truth is that you took their words and attitude into your brain; processed them, and gave yourself permission to set your feelings aside and adopt others' negative behavior. Anger, sadness, jealousy, greed, and happiness are all emotions that you choose and control. You should choose a good and positive attitude daily.

There are negative people all around us; they try to influence our emotions and attitudes daily. They talk about others constantly; they blame someone else because they are having a bad day. When they are feeling miserable, they want you to feel miserable. Because "misery loves company," a negative person may target you, and if they sense you are weak, they will try to bring you down to their level. Sad as it may seem, having something in common with another, even if it is negative, often seems better than being miserable alone.

For many years, I have talked to young adults in high schools, and I've always stressed that success is about attitude. I explain to them that another's attitude need not affect theirs. I tell them that when someone comes up to you and calls you fat or ugly, stupid or dumb, look them right in the eye and say, "Thank you for noticing, and have a great day!" You may be laughing at that idea, but seriously, negative people need to and want to get inside your head and bring you down to their level. When they say destructive things to you, if you respond with positive energy and excitement, they are surprised and taken aback. Chances are that they will not bother you again because they recognize you as a positive person, someone not influenced by their negativity, and they will move on to seek out a weaker, more vulnerable target, someone who will accept their ridicule and belittling. This works the same in the business world as it does in your personal life.

If you remember one thing from this book, I want you to remember this: "To whatever you give your energy or time, it will grow, flourish, and prosper in your life. To whatever you deny your energy or time, it will wither, die, and leave your life."

As an example, negative people do not associate with me because I am a positive person, and my energy is positive; therefore, the negativity in other people cannot flourish when they are around me, thus leaving them feeling no real association or connection with me. They will either be charged by my positive energy and remain, or they retain their negativity and move on.

Likewise, because I give my positive energy to my goals and ambitions, they tend to grow and flourish in my life.

How often have you begun your day only to realize that it is not going well? Often, I'm sure. With YOU being the "I" in team, you can choose to continue and just get through the day, or you can choose to "create a great day for yourself!" Some days seem like it is a constant battle, and you have to "win the day." There is nothing wrong with, and very much right with, putting forth effort to create a great day! When you write your salutation at the end of your letters or emails, write, "Create a great day for yourself," or "Win the day." Then notice how it effects and changes attitudes, including your own.

A positive attitude is essential if you choose to be happy or "successful on purpose." Train yourself to be positive. Go one day without saying anything negative. When you have accomplished that, go one day without allowing yourself to think a negative thought. When you have been successful for an entire day, go two days and then three. Soon you will have learned to think, speak, and react positively and your entire world will be changed forever.

I know that all you have to do is sit in the lunchroom at work or the coffee shop to tell me that what I am asking you to do is not easy if there are a lot of people around you being negative all the time. Here is where the power of attitude comes into play. I look at this as a chance for you to be a leader. Someone has to be a leader, why not you? The market is open on positive attitudes, and

Attitude

if you haven't noticed, there isn't a lot of competition. How many times have you heard those around you at work complain about pay, benefits, or people with whom they work and blah blah blah? These are the same people who complain that the sun is too bright on a clear day and then complain there is no sunshine when it is cloudy. See the pattern?

During my first week as the Director of Safety and Employee Development for a Midwest based packaging company, I was meeting with some employees to discuss the safety culture and potential improvements. I was talking about the positive ideas and concepts that I would like to implement. Several of the employees did not pull any punches as they told me that they had heard all this before and that it wouldn't last. Well, everyone always seems to know what the problems are, but few offer solutions to fix them. Why? It is easy to complain because there is minimal ownership, whereas solutions require ownership and energy to act. As the meeting continued, one individual continued to complain about everything, so it seemed. I thought that he had gone on long enough, so I interjected and asked him if he had walked by one day, tripped in the front door, and accidentally filled out his job application, or if he had filled it out on purpose? He was pretty much done complaining at that point since I required him to take ownership in what he was saying.

If you accept your job on purpose, you make an agreement with your employer. That agreement is that you show up for work and perform to the best of your ability; the employer, in turn, compensates you for your efforts. All other benefits are also expressed to you at this time if there are any. No surprises. Seems simple enough.

If you believe that you are the "I in team and that you are your greatest asset, you only have a couple of options if you are not happy with your job or career. One, you must take positive action to make it better, or two, you need to get a different job or career because you are too special to spend forty hours a week unhappy and negative. Either option is a win-win situation for both parties involved.

Negative attitudes and negative energy create negative results. Positive attitudes and positive energy create positive results. Controlling your attitude will make the rest of your life the best of your life.

Yes, it is that simple.

Toolbox Takeaway:

To whatever you give your energy, it will grow, flourish, and prosper in your life. To whatever you deny your energy, it will wither, die, and leave your life.

Below, list five areas in your life you would like to dedicate more energy/time to.

1. _____

2. _____

3. _____

4. _____

5. _____

Now, list five items in your life that you should not be spending as much energy/time on.

1. _____

2. _____

3. _____

4. _____

5. _____

GOALS

*"You could be anything you want to be;
you just have to want to be."*

R. Saint

GOALS

Do you want to reach your goals? Are you ready to take the steps necessary to reach them? If your answer is yes, then stop committing actions every day that are taking you further from your goals.

If, at last, you are ready to make that commitment to not only set goals, but also achieve them, then do it! It is as simple as it sounds.

You, like many others, have probably set goals in the past, but failed to set in place a strategy or a plan to achieve them. A goal without a plan is no more than a wish, and a wish is no more than a dream. Neither requires energy or emotion. For example: In a minute, I'll ask you to close your eyes and let your imagination take you away to a place where you wish you could be, where time has no limits. When you are there, allow yourself to experience the conditions around you. Imagine the mist from the gentle breeze as it brushes your face, and hear the seagulls in the distance as you walk along a beach just before dawn. Imagine the sting of the bitter cold as you're racing down the slopes of a mountain. Smell the steaming cup of cocoa, and feel the welcoming flames in the fireplace that await to warm and relax you back at the lodge. Choose your very own place, but try to feel and imagine the conditions around you. Now, close your eyes for a few seconds, and dream.

Your eyes are open now. Are you there at that wonderful place?

Of course, you are not! You are not there because you didn't do anything other than dream; there was no plan or action set in motion to get you there. All you did was wish that you were there, and all by itself, a wish or a dream will get you nowhere.

Another reason why you cannot reach your goals is because your commitment changes. When you first set a goal, whether it is to shed those unwanted pounds or open a savings account that you have been putting off, you go into it very focused and excited. You're pumped and can't wait to start, right? Unfortunately, for most people, it is shortly after this point that they begin to lose focus, and the conviction of their goals is not strong enough to get them to the end. If that describes you, in your life and with your goal setting, you should not waste another minute of your time and energy because you are only setting yourself up for failure "on purpose." Once you've set your goal, but before you begin, you need to ask yourself this question: "How bad do I really want what I say that I want?"

A story that I heard long ago relates well to my point on goals. A young man from Chicago came to Wisconsin for a week of duck hunting. Though he had been extremely excited about spending this week in Southwest Wisconsin, his excitement gradually dwindled by the sixth day as he once again sat in the river bottoms without so much as seeing one duck.

On the seventh day, he was actually debating with himself whether or not he should go out for the last day of hunting;

however, the thought of his friends laughing if he showed up back in the city with no duck was enough to get him up by four a.m. and out by his tree to sit yet another day in hopes of seeing a duck.

By three o'clock that afternoon, feeling totally miserable and sickly, he was ready to give it up when he saw a duck fly above him. He quickly took aim, fired, and hit the duck. Excited now, he grabbed his gear and set out to track the fallen duck. A good distance later he came to a fence line, and about twenty feet on the other side, lay the duck with an elderly farmer standing over it. The young hunter asked the farmer to kindly toss the bird over the fence, and he'd be on his way. The farmer looked at him and asked, "Young man, see that fence there? That is my fence, and anything on this side of it is mine; therefore, the duck belongs to me." Tired and irritated by now, the young man said, "Look, old man, I've been out here for seven days; I feel miserable, and I should be in the hospital. I know that I shot that duck a ways back, so give it to me, and I'll leave and be out of your way."

The old man said, "Look, son, you're in Wisconsin now, so let's settle it the way we settle things here. We'll fight for the duck, and the best man wins." The young man, looking the old man over, thinks to himself, "This should be easy. This old man is no match for my youth and strength." He jumps over the fence, puts up his fists, and says, "let's go old man." The farmer responds, "Not so fast, young one; this is my land, so I get the first punch." The young man, thinking this feeble old man can't have much of a punch says, "Take your best shot." The farmer pulls up his overalls, steps back, and launches forward, driving his right foot into the young man's groin. He drops to the ground, rolling around in pain. After a few minutes, the young man gets his strength back, gets to his feet, puts his fists up, and says, "Alright, old man, now it is my turn," but before the young man could take a swing, the old man says, "Hold on, son; you can have the duck."

The moral of the story is that when you have a goal in your life, you better be prepared to get kicked in the groin along the way because goals are not easy. People will try to stop you, and goals ALWAYS have a cost. If a goal is worth it to you, its gain will outweigh the costs, and it will be worth your effort in dealing with the obstacles. Are you willing to put up with setbacks or conflicts along the way? Again, the question you must ask yourself is, "How badly do I want what I say that I want?"

Believe it or not, you are exactly where you have worked to be. That's right. Whatever your age is, you are right where you are as a result of what you have said, thought, and done in your life, right up to the last decision that you have made, maybe even as recent as ten minutes ago. As an example, let's look at the goal we talked about earlier; losing weight. First, why is losing weight a goal? Barring any medical issues, most people are overweight because they are overeating, eating the wrong foods, and not exercising to burn the energy (calories), that they put into their body. Many people live to eat instead of eat to live. Your mindset should be that food is fuel for your body's engine, so what kind of fuel do you want to use to keep your vehicle (body) running great?

To be successful on purpose, you must take care of and nurture your mind and body to operate at maximum efficiency. I have never accidentally eaten a double cheeseburger or hot fudge sundae. I have done it with pure intent! We must take responsibility for our actions and always remember that we are a result of what we say, think, and do.

Too many people just expect their body to work and support them every day without taking care of it. For most, this will work for a while until the body (and mind) breaks down because it has been abused and neglected, and then the medical issues surface. Yeah, I know what you're saying to yourself right now. "We are all going to fall apart eventually, and I feel good now, so what's the big deal?" The big deal is that YOU are your greatest asset, and as the "I" in team, you need to maximize your potential; you must care for your mind and body to nurture your spirit and attitude.

During a conversation with a woman at a speaking engagement in Iowa years ago, I asked her what she felt her greatest asset was. She responded that her children were her greatest assets. I told her straight up that she needed to change her attitude. That was not what she wanted to hear! Seriously, I explained, when I owned a health club, there were always a few moms who would tell me how much they would like to join the club, but they were too busy getting their son to basketball and their daughter to volleyball. They just couldn't find the time. My response to these moms was always, "One of these days, your son may be riding his bike to basketball, and your daughter may be walking to volleyball because you are dead. Why? You didn't think that it was important to take care of yourself." Listen up all you moms, your children want you to take time to take care of yourself because they love you and because they want you to be around for them to love and enjoy for many years to come. Same for you dads too, get off the couch!

There is an old proverb that says, "A man too busy to take care of his body is like a mechanic too busy to take care of his tools."

Let's get back to goals. You've seen the ads on television "Are you tired of starving yourself just to lose a pound or two? Well, no more! Now, you can lose weight simply by taking our miracle pill." "Be your own boss; work from home only two or three hours a day, and make thousands of dollars effortlessly." And of course there are those that sell...secrets. "With our secrets, you can buy million dollar homes for only pennies on the dollar."

The one bit of information that they never tell you is that there is ALWAYS a cost to any goal. The cost may be time away from your family. Maybe while your co-workers or friends are out having fun, you are alone working towards your goal. As you are developing your strategy or plan for your goal, you need to also consider the potential costs if you are to be successful on purpose. Of course, the gain or the value to you should always exceed the cost, or you should not pursue the goal.

This true and inspiring story is about setting and reaching goals. A young girl, whom I will call Joanna, decided in ninth grade that she wanted to go to college. This was no small goal because her family was a family of average means, living in rural America and getting by from paycheck to paycheck, as many families seem to do in these areas. Joanna realized that the only way she would be able to reach this goal was to do her very best in school and hopefully earn a scholarship. Her "friends" gave her the nickname, "No-no Joanna," because, throughout her high school years when they invited her to go to parties on the weekends, she would say, "No, I have to study." When boyfriends would try to pressure her into sex by saying everyone is doing it, she would say, "No, I am not everyone." To make a long story short, Joanna stayed true to her strategy and goal, and four years later was awarded a full scholarship to a major university. Was there a cost to her goal? Sure! It cost her many fun nights with her friends; it cost her several boyfriends because she was not like everyone else. Was the gain greater than the cost for Joanna? Well, she went on to school, earned a degree, and now has a career doing what she wants to be doing. That, my friend, is being successful on purpose!

Joanna understood that she is the "I" in team and her success was directly related to her commitment to "her." To have that discipline, focus, and passion at such a young age is special, but it does not matter what your age is when it comes to your commitment to your goals. If you have focus, self-discipline, and passion, you will very likely end up exactly where you want to be.

Goals

If you want to reach your goals, it is time to start doing what you know you need to do; make the commitment, develop a strategy, (include the potential costs), pursue the goal with passion, and ask yourself daily, "How bad do I really want what I say that I want?"

Toolbox takeaway:

A goal without a plan is no more than a wish, and a wish is no more than a dream; neither requires energy or emotion.

Below, set a goal for your self; include a strategy to reach it and the potential costs.

_____

_____

_____

_____

_____

_____

It's Great to Be You!

COMMITMENT

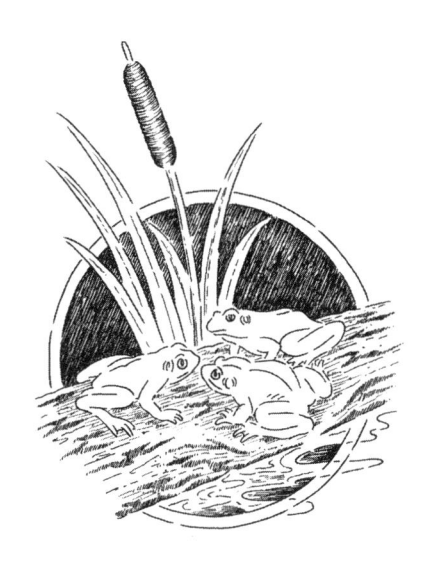

Three frogs are sitting on a log and one decides to jump off; how many frogs are left sitting on the log? When you have the answer, turn the page....

COMMITMENT

You probably said that there are two frogs sitting on the log, but actually there are three. You see, if you read carefully you will realize that one frog made the decision to jump off, he didn't follow the decision with an action. I'm sure that you have made decisions at different times in your life, perhaps to start a savings account, go on that much wanted vacation, shed those unwanted pounds, or volunteer more of your time. However, just making those decisions was not making a commitment to see them through. Doing any one the above, or for that matter, being happy, achieving goals, and being successful on purpose, require commitment, a commitment to YOU, the "I" in team. Once you choose a goal, put a strategy in place to achieve it, and take action, you have made a commitment to see it through and bring it to fruition.

"Commitment" means to choose a goal, establish a strategy, and then not "renegotiate the standard" with yourself. If you are committed to that goal, you cannot justify to yourself why it is okay to fail. I am sure that you have done that at one time or another. You set a goal, and then when you are about two thirds of the way to your goal, you decide that it is "good enough." You even praised yourself for getting so far before you quit. For example: You are painting a wall, and you know that to be done right, it needs three coats of paint. However, you get tired and bored with painting so you make a decision to cut corners and decide that two coats will be enough. Cutting corners only sets you up for "failure on purpose." Cutting corners keeps you from reaching your potential. Do you know what the worst part is? You will spend much energy and emotion convincing yourself that it is acceptable.

Winners, champions, leaders, and warriors understand that cutting corners and quitting is not acceptable! As the "I" in team it is imperative that you understand that your commitment to YOU is of paramount importance. As I stated in the beginning, the opportunities available to you are in direct relation to your commitment to you. Once the reality of that statement sets in, it should excite you beyond your wildest imagination.

Commitment is one component that separates winners, champions, leaders, and warriors from quitters, losers, and whiners. It is a commitment to self-maximization and a standard of excellence that will lead to your personal success.

It's Great to Be You!

<u>*Toolbox takeaway*</u>:

Commitment means to choose a goal, establish a strategy, and then not "renegotiate the standard" with yourself.

Below, list areas in your life you have made a commitment to and realized success. Take time and experience the feelings of those successes.

_____

_____

_____

_____

_____

_____

_____

_____

_____

_____

_____

STANDARD OF EXCELLENCE

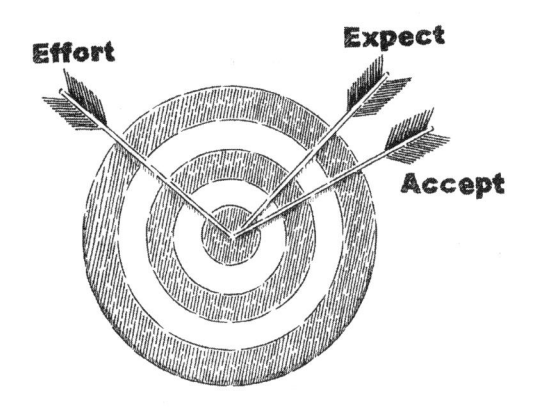

"Although energy levels may change on any given day, effort must remain a constant."

R. Saint

STANDARD OF EXCELLENCE

A personal standard of excellence truly takes commitment. As with success, reaching your goals and having a great attitude do not come by accident. A personal standard of excellence is developed 100% on purpose.

Anyone can be average. This takes no special skills or effort. No one rewards average effort. However, if you want to reach, as well as maximize, your full potential, you must decide to be extraordinary and take action to make it happen. This is not as drastic as it may seem because "extra-ordinary" is simply more than ordinary. You could call it "average plus." Extraordinary is taking one more step after everyone else has quit. It is one more hour of practice when everyone else has said good enough, or it is calling on one more potential customer than the other salespeople did. Do you see a pattern here? Extraordinary effort will yield extraordinary results. A standard of excellence is setting yourself up for success by keeping what you expect and what you accept in line with each other.

When people talk about culture such as creating a culture of safety in the workplace or creating a positive culture in the company, community, or even your household, they are purposely creating and developing an environment in which they want to function. The way to change a culture or maintain a culture is to have set expectations, and what you accept cannot deviate from these standards.

You need to pay close attention here as this often is the difference between success and failure, personally and professionally, and it often goes unnoticed until it is too late. Many companies will set a standard, what they expect from their employees in their job functions such as productivity, safety, or quality. The trouble begins when you accept less than you expect.

Let's say at work that you are expected to have a ninety-five percent quality rate on your product, however, you are under a tight deadline to get the product out the door. You make a decision to accept an eighty-five percent quality rate instead of standing by your previous commitment of ninety-five percent. You have just set yourself up for failure on purpose. If you expect ninety-five percent and you accept eighty-five percent, people will give you eighty-five percent because you have made it acceptable. However, if you expect ninety-five percent and will only accept ninety-five percent; that is what people will give you. This concept may also be applied when you expect a certain level of competence from yourself or others in your family.

There are three "wants" I know to be true:
1. People do not want to be yelled at.
2. People do not want to fail.
3. People want to have a value.

People would rather be complimented than scolded. They would rather succeed than fail, and all people want to have a value; people want to know that their efforts matter and that the space they take up has a purpose.

As you set a standard of excellence for yourself, know that you must always focus on keeping what you expect and what you accept in line with each other. The following is an example that I have used in my martial arts schools for many years. You can use this in any area of your life. I challenge my students with a question like this: Let's say that "you" come to class on Monday and give your "very best effort"; then, "you" come to class on Tuesday and give your "lesser" effort. Which "you" or which "effort" is going to show up on Wednesday? The truth is that you do not know.

It may have been that you were tired, maybe you just had a low energy level day; we all have them. However, that should have nothing to do with your effort. When you, the "I" in team, set a standard of excellence for yourself, understand that your effort must be "constant." This means that whatever you have to give, you must always give the best of it. This is how I explain it to my students; "being tired does not give you permission to perform a technique incorrectly! It means there may not be as much power or speed behind your performance, but you are still expected to do it correctly."

The same holds true in the workplace. You may be tired or perhaps not feel well, but that does not allow you to cut corners or do an inferior job. When you give your best effort, regardless of physical energy level or mental fatigue, you are setting yourself up for success on purpose.

Your mind harbors what your body manifests (your mind controls your body). Therefore, if you set your "best" effort as your standard, your mind and body will not tune into anything other than your best. They will not recognize laziness or half efforts. Your mind and body do not care what you put into them, but you need to realize that you will not get any more out of either of them than what you have deposited.

Always remember to control what you can control, and do not try to control what you cannot, as this will lead to frustration, stress, and quite frankly, a gross waste of your valuable time. Accepting only what you expect is setting a high standard of excellence for yourself and truly setting yourself up for success on purpose. Pretty simple, huh?

Toolbox takeaway:

Your mind and body do not care what you put into them, but you need to realize that you will not get anymore out of either of them than what you have deposited.

Start today. Below, list areas in your life that you want to be "extra" ordinary.

_____

_____

_____

It's Great to Be You!

FOCUS & SELF DISCIPLINE

"Never forget from where you came, and always remember where you are going."

R. Saint

FOCUS & SELF DISCIPLINE

Elsewhere in this book, I talked about commitment and goals. I have also told you that goals without plans are merely wishes and dreams, and neither of the two will get you anywhere unless they are combined with energy and action. Focus and self-discipline are also important and powerful tools, which are essential elements in committing yourself to achieving goals in your life. The direction in which you focus your energy is even more important. Ask yourself these questions:

Am I committed to my goals?

How often do I focus my energy on my goals?

What actions do I allow that prevent me from working consistently towards my goals?

Identifying the answers to these questions is important because the answers are the roadblocks, either real or perceived, that will prevent you from concentrating your energy on your goals and successfully reaching them.

The approach of football season here in the Midwest is probably very similar to that in any other part of the country when it comes to the fervent dedication of the fans to their favorite teams. Like clockwork, around September each year, emotions begin to rev up, excitement and anticipation set in, and "pigskin fever" strikes! Men (especially) find the "game" at the forefront of every conversation. The buzz and hum at the coffee machines, the elevated pitch in conversation around the water coolers, and in the sports bars and pubs, seems to infect even the most timid of football fans. Before you know it, whether you are a full blown "sack-attack maniac" or an innocent person just happening by who gets caught up in all the hype, the plans and the festivities begin to take shape, and no one can wait for the big day. The big day of course - football Sunday!

I will use this "football euphoria" to make my point about focus. On Monday mornings the conversation is all about the games the past weekend. The plays are run and re-run over and over. Everyone is well aware of how each individual would have made that play had he been the one in the game himself. Tuesday rolls around, and it is pretty much agreed that the last game is over, time to put it away because the plans for the upcoming game are already taking on a life of their own. Some parties will go the whole nine yards with a pre-game cookout, drinks, and snacks during the game. Another might serve beer and snacks during the first half with pizza and finger foods during the half time show. Each week is guaranteed to be a bigger, more fun, and food filled fest than the last, right up to the big day when it kicks up several notches and the "boastful bowls" begin. The goal setting, the energy, and action committed to these parties is remarkable to say the least.

As the weekend draws nearer, once again the intensity builds,

It's Great to Be You!

and the excitement level makes it evident that nothing will get in the way of this week's "football mania." The food and snack menus are coming together as to who will bring what; the little maps to your home or the favorite sports bar of choice are printed, and the invitation list is now overflowing. The "pitbull" effort to coordinate and bring the upcoming weekend's game to an even greater climax than the last is on! Much time and planning have been lavished on these game parties, and the anticipation and excitement of their success is so important that no amount of commitment or action needed to reach the intended goal is too much.

Fast forward to "game day!" Your wife has asked you to do a couple of odds and ends around the house, but it seems that the anticipation of the game and your full concentration to the excitement of the pre-game analysts have caused you to come down with a case of selective hearing. You finally respond that you don't have time to get at them today, but you will get to it first thing tomorrow. As you listen to the pre-game analysts and they set you up for what they expect today's game to look like, you find yourself disagreeing with them. Under your breath, while mumbling your disagreement, you become fairly vocal towards the television screen. You cannot focus on anything that does not have to do with the party and the game, and it is quite obvious to your spouse by now that you are committed only to football Sunday!

The big day is here, and guests have arrived. People are

socializing, and an air of excitement is felt throughout the room. The food and drinks rock, adrenalin is pumping, and the game has just begun. Suddenly, out of nowhere, your team misses a very important play, and immediately you and your friends are out of your seats, angrily rebuking and scolding the "idiot" on the television screen, who in reality, is actually in a stadium half way across the country and he wouldn't really care what you think even if he could hear you! However, that does not prevent all of you from continuing your tirade at the unyielding, inanimate piece of furniture, the TV, as to why that player should not be paid to play football in the first place!

They cut to a commercial, and you all continue to argue about how they need to play someone the next time who, at the least, knows something about football. Of course, the play was rehashed at least a dozen times during the commercial, and you are all in agreement that anyone of you is smarter than that idiot that bungled it.

The commercial is over, and the game is again in progress. Wouldn't you know it, but the same guy who "screwed up" just a few plays ago makes an ingenious play to redeem himself. All of you are back on your feet, fists in the air, screaming once again at the still unaffected television screen about what a genius move it was when they traded to get this "brilliant athlete" on your team, and he still cannot hear you.

Then what followed was an example of misdirected focus

when the game and plays weren't going the way that you thought they should. You began the useless act of wasting energy by jumping up and down and yelling at a television set. You need to realize that, no matter how much you scream and yell when something goes against your desired outcome; it will not change the fact that you have no control over it whatsoever.

If you want yelling at someone to make a difference in the outcome of reaching your goals next time, walk into the bathroom, look into the mirror and yell at that person. The person whom you see in the mirror can control his/her words, thoughts, and actions. Through focus and self-discipline, that person can direct his/her commitment of valuable time, effort, and energy towards reaching his/her personal goals.

You've probably realized by now that I am trying to draw a parallel to show our desire and ability to exert energy and action to bring about the outcomes we find most important in our everyday lives. Imagine the success that you would realize if you would give this kind of commitment and energy to your own personal life goals for yourself or your family! Starting on Monday, you would be looking at where you went wrong earlier. By Tuesday, you would be beginning to implement a strategy that would help you reach your goal (the party). Soon after, the commitment would be made, which was, the energy and action invested in making menus, placing phone calls, going to the grocery store and liquor depot, and all of the other careful planning and checkpoints set up to insure the upcoming party's success. Nearly a solid week of commitment went into assuring the success of this goal.

Thought: Do you put this type of focus, commitment, and energy into your personal life goals?

Am I saying that you should not have a party on football Sunday? Absolutely not! Fill up the ice trays, load up the charcoal and brats and hunker down for a family and friend fun-filled experience. However, I am using this analogy to make the point that many people focus their energies in the wrong direction (away from their goals) and then wonder why they do not reach them. Remember from the goals chapter - all goals have a cost, and it is up to you to decide if you want to meet that cost, which may mean missing the game!

Once again, I want to remind you that you need to focus on what you can control and not try to control that which you cannot. To set goals and have strategies in place to reach them are not enough. The focus must be in the right direction.

It's Great to Be You!

<u>*Toolbox takeaway*</u>:

Am I committed to my goals? How often do I focus my energy on my goals? What actions do I allow that prevent me from working towards my goals?

Focused energy will yield results. Below, log your successes as they occur.

SUCCESS

"You must understand failure before
you can realize success."

B. Franklin

SUCCESS

During speaking engagements, I often ask my audience, "By a show of hands, how many of you do not want to be successful?" I have never seen a hand raised. Why? Because everyone no matter his or her goal in life, wants to be successful. But, what is success, and how is it measured? To some, success is having the most toys; to others, it may be to have the most money; others may measure their success in having mental, physical, emotional, or even spiritual health.

YOU are your own greatest asset. When is the last time that you developed a strategy for who you are, where you're going, what you want, and how you are going to get it? You must ask and answer those four questions before you can begin your journey towards being successful "on purpose."

This is my question for you: "Do you believe that you have the ability to become successful?" You may have heard many times that "if you want something bad enough, you will acquire it," but you never thought that it could pertain to you. Well, it can, and it will if you begin to focus on your greatest asset - YOU. Let's take a look at you and ask some questions that need to be answered honestly before we can begin our journey of empowering you.

I call this a personal evaluation or an attitude assessment test. You need to rate yourself from 1 to 5 with 5 being the "most proficient" and 1 being the "least proficient." Write your scores next to each question, and this will give you an idea of where you rate now, as well as what areas you will need to work on towards reaching your personal development goals.

> Do I have specific goals?
> Can I take discouragement?
> Do I have a strategy in place?
> Do I express myself with conviction?
> Do people understand what I have to say?
> Do I give people an impression of helpfulness?
> Do I talk to the point without a tendency to ramble?
> Are my tasks completed when due, or do I procrastinate?
> Am I alert for any ideas that might help me improve myself?
> Do I have complete faith in my abilities? Do I believe in myself?
> Do I take at least five hours a week for my personal development?

Each question asks you to do something to which you may not be accustomed to: they ask you to look at and be accountable to you. Now that you have evaluated yourself and have an idea of your personal level of self-awareness, let's move forward, improve on the lower scores, and enhance the higher ones.

What you believe your personal value is to the world, to the people in your life, and to you will directly affect your success. What is your value on a day when everything went just as you expected, or perhaps better? How about days when everything falls into place and you accomplish so much you are able to start on tomorrow's tasks and maybe even take Friday off? Would your value differ on a day when everything goes wrong, when it feels as though the entire world hates you, or you're late for all your appointments, your computer breaks down, and everyone needs something from you?

Bob was a very successful man, a billionaire who had just purchased fifteen hundred acres of property in Arizona. This property had flat lands, several streams, and some hilly regions. Bob, being rightfully proud of his recent acquisition, invited a few of his millionaire friends there to show off his newest investment.

Bob rented a few SUV's and took his friends on a site seeing tour of his property. At noon, they headed back to the house, an enormous house with an Olympic sized swimming pool, seemingly out of place in the middle of nowhere, but an undoubtedly, welcomingly seclusive for a billionaire. As they neared the back of the house and the pool area, they noticed that the magnificent pool was filled with alligators. One of Bob's friends, chuckling and exchanging glances with the others, got the nerve to ask, "Say, Bob, what's with all the alligators in your pool?" Bob explained, "I believe alligators are a symbol of courage, and it is courage that has made me the success I am today. I believe that it is courage that will help me continue my success. As a matter of fact, I offer any one of you this challenge. If you have the courage to jump into the pool, swim to the other side, and come out alive, I will give you anything that I have obtained throughout my lifetime: my money, my home, my land, you name it."

Bob's friends, smiling and thanking him while declining his offer, headed to the house for lunch, when suddenly, they heard a splash. They looked back in horror to see one of their friend's frantically swimming across the pool as the alligators were closing in on him. So scared that he could hardly breathe, Bob's friend made it to the other side and climbed out, a little shaken, but very much alive. The friends were all amazed, and Bob was truly astonished. Bob walked over to his friend and asked, "Sir, you are a tremendous man of courage, and I am a man of my word. Which of my possessions do you desire?" The friend, totally exhausted and still gasping for air, looked up at Bob and said, "I have only one request." "Yes, and that is?" Bob asked. The man looked at Bob and said, "I want to know who pushed me into the pool back there!"

The moral of the story is that situations are not always as they seem. The world does not wake up and decide to hate you. It's called a bad day, and everyone has them. How you react to that day is in direct relation to what you think your true value is to the world.

It's Great to Be You!

<u>*Toolbox takeaway*</u>:

Develop a strategy for who you are, where you're going, what you want, and how you're going to get it.

Below, list what success is to you?

_____

_____

_____

_____

_____

_____

_____

_____

_____

_____

_____

_____

SUCCESS TRIANGLE

"Be successful on purpose!"

R. Saint

SUCCESS TRAINGLE

Over and over I hear people give every reason (excuse) why they cannot be successful or achieve their goals. It is either that they don't have the money to make their ideas reality or that they are too busy with everything else in their life. They don't have time to pursue the one goal they really want to achieve. It really comes down to your commitment to what you want. You have heard this and will continue to hear it throughout the entire book, and it is the question that gets right to the heart of your commitment - "How bad do you really want what you say you want?"

This example came to me about eight years ago when I attended the Arnold Schwartzenegger Fitness Festival in Ohio. I owned a health club at the time and had taught martial arts for eighteen years. I believe it was the first year that martial arts were included in the event, so it was an exciting event to attend.

I was beginning to sell fitness apparel at my center, and there was a vendor there that was selling the workout pants that were becoming the hot item in the industry. They were the pants that body builders were wearing, which looked something like the parachute pants of the day with all kinds of multi-colored fabric. The individual who was selling the pants was a man that had moved to the United States. He could hardly speak English, as he had been in the States for only a short period of time. He was the owner of this new company that he had always envisioned. After a few long, hard minutes of trying to communicate with him, I purchased several cases of these clothes for my club. I returned to the club later that week and began to sell the clothes that sold rather quickly due to the fact that no one else in the area had been selling these yet, so we were on the leading edge of the curve.

The real story here is that this gentleman sold out of many of the sizes that he brought with him well before the end of the conference, as other people, just as I did, thought these pants were a great value. The owner was trying his best to communicate to every customer. He was extremely successful despite having to overcome one of the most difficult barriers in the world, the communication barrier.

Why, then, was he able to sell so many clothes? I believe it was because he applied what I call the "Success Triangle." You may know of the fire triangle, which illustrates that a fire cannot exist without three elements present. These three elements are heat, fuel, and oxygen. A fire cannot exist without all three of these elements present. The success triangle is also made up of three elements. These elements are Motive, Desire, and Opportunity. You must have these three elements working together to achieve success on purpose. You can have opportunity and motive, but without desire, you will not be successful. You can have desire and opportunity, but without motive, you will not be successful. You can have motive and desire, but without having or creating opportunity, you will not be successful. It's as simple as that.

The owner of this new clothing company, who had recently moved to this country to pursue his passion of running a company, had all three elements working for him. He had the desire or passion to start this company. He had the motive or reason, which he showed by moving to this country to pursue the American dream, and last and certainly not least, he created the opportunity. Whether he knew it or not, this man was not successful by accident; it was completely on purpose. If you have grown up in this country and speak english, stop whining and complaining that you cannot make it for whatever reason because it is a cop out. Apply the success triangle elements to your goals and ambitions, and watch your goals become a reality in your life.

PERSEVERANCE

Perseverance is one of the most important tools that you can have in your success toolbox. As the "I in team, you know that perseverance is an essential tool in reaching your goals. Why? Because you understand that all goals will have a cost and if you are not willing to pay that cost, you will probably give up as soon as adversity sets in because it is more comfortable to do so.

One example of perseverance that always comes to mind for me is Thomas Edison. One of his inventions was the light bulb. One of the stories that circulate about Mr. Edison and his light bulb idea is that a reporter once said to him, "Thomas, why don't you give up this silly idea for this light bulb? You have tried over five thousand different experiments to make it work, and you have failed. As the story goes, Mr. Edison looked the reporter in the eye and said, "Failed! I have successfully identified over five thousand ways that do not work!" This sentence says a lot about the power of tools for success, such as attitude, focus, discipline, and perseverance. Thomas Edison did not look at the failed experiments as failures. On the contrary, he saw them as opportunities. He truly understood that he was the "I" in team and that it was his belief in himself that would lead to his successes. He figured that every time he tried an experiment that did not work, he was one step closer to the one that would work. Where would we be today if Thomas would have listened to this reporter and given up?

Imagine for a moment that you are Thomas Edison and that you have this great idea. You walk a mile down the forest road to your neighbor's cabin and knock on his door. As you enter his humble home, you begin to tell him that he can throw all of his candles away because you have this great, new invention that will change his life forever. You are going to take this "thing" you call a light bulb and screw it into this other "thing" you call a socket. You are going to attach two wires to it and run them across the ceiling and down the wall; you are then going to attach these two wires to a "thing" you call a switch. When this switch is in the up position, you will have all this wonderful light, and when it is down, it will be pitch dark. What do you think your friend in the humble little cabin would say to you? My guess is that he would look at you like you have been working too hard and are in need of a vacation. More likely, he would say that you are losing your mind and that you need to go back home, get some rest and then plan to see a doctor!

Just think, the combustible engine, the television, digital pictures, computers, and the list goes on and on with inventions whose creators were probably laughed at and ridiculed for this "stupid idea that will never catch on." If the inventor, or "I" in team, were to quit every time someone told her that she was crazy, many of the great inventions we have today would not be here. We would still be burning candles possibly if Edison listened to the naysayer. By the way, Thomas Edison was afraid of the dark, which I am guessing was one of his motivations for inventing the light bulb.

Michael Jordan was cut from his basketball team as a freshman in high school because he was told he was not good enough to make the team. What if HE would have believed that he was not good enough and given up? There are endless stories. I am sure you have some of your own, which make the point that we need to believe in ourselves unconditionally first and foremost.

Any person I can think of to whom I admire for his/her accomplishments has had to overcome some level of adversity along the way. You're too short, you're too fat, you're not smart enough, you're too nice etc.… Let's take a look at the "you're not smart enough" comment. Do you realize that some of the smartest people in the world with the highest IQ's can't hold down a regular job or converse with average people in a coffee shop? You do not have to be the most traditionally educated person to be the most successful person. Is it a positive accomplishment for you if you have a master's degree or your doctorate in whatever field of study you chose? Yes, of course it is. Is it a requirement that you possess these degrees to be successful? No, of course it is not. What is required, however, is Motive, Desire, and Opportunity: the success triangle.

I often interchange the word "desire" with the word "passion." Passion is more important than knowledge when pursuing your goals and successes. Steve Jobs, the cofounder of Apple Computers, dropped out of college to pursue his passion. Bill Gates, the cofounder of Microsoft, dropped out of college to pursue his passion. These two, as well as a few others really changed the world, as we know it today. Both of them had the Motive, Desire, and Opportunity to maximize their true potential.

I was speaking at a technical college to a group of young entrepreneurs along with several academic instructors a few years back, and a couple of the instructors took offense to my statement that passion is more important than knowledge when pursuing your goals. That is fine, as I enjoy a good exchange of ideas and beliefs; however, they were unable to convince me to believe otherwise. As an entrepreneur myself and owner of three different businesses that I started from the ground up, I feel confident that I can talk about this with credibility. Consultants told me that I would need to have a population base of at least 75,000 to 100,000 people to operate a fitness center like the one I envisioned. The fitness industry at that time said that if you had ½ to 1% of your population using your club, you were doing very well. I owned and operated the fitness center I envisioned in a community of 3,400 people and at one time had 10% of the population using my center. I operated the center for ten years and was profitable by the second year. I had Motive, Desire, and Opportunity.

You see, you can have all the knowledge in the world, but without passion, you will find it very difficult to reach your goals. There are many billion-dollar businesses and inventions that never happened for people who had all the knowledge necessary, but lacked the passion to see it through. They decided to start a business, but did not have the passion to commit to it. However, if you are passionate about your goals, you will gain the knowledge because you are committed to action.

One of the biggest obstacles that you face is having others not only telling you it can't be done, but also working to prove to you it cannot be done. Many times these people are your friends. That's right; I said your friends. I've said this earlier–most people around you are not happy, and they do not want to see you happy either. Your friends may not even realize that they are doing this because the society that we live in today almost applauds failure and scorns success. I mean, really, take a moment and look through the daily newspaper and count how many positive articles you come across versus the number of negative articles on any given day. This is exactly why you must trust in yourself, the "I" in team, and do not let negative influences into your brain.

The good news is this - with all the negative influences and forces that face you every day, there is hope. For every negative action, energy or force, there is an equal and opposite one. It is an unbending natural law. As the "I" in team you should see this as an opportunity, not an impediment.

As you go about setting goals, developing strategies, and changing your life on purpose, you should always ask yourself if the success triangle is part of that plan; if it is not, get ready because it may hurt!

Toolbox takeaway:

You can have all the knowledge in the world, but without passion, you will find it hard to reach your goal.

Below, list the positive influences in your life.

_____

_____

_____

_____

_____

It's Great to Be You!

STRESS

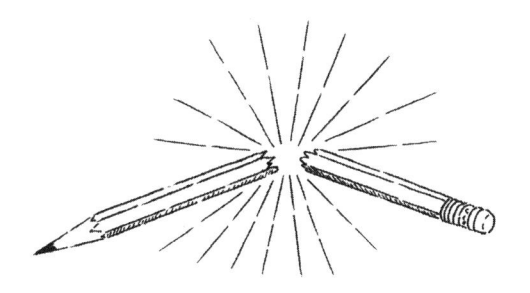

*"All the worry in the world
won't change a thing."*

B. Jack

STRESS

One definition of stress is the inability of an organism to function in its present environment. When you are "stressed out," how do you function? The answer is that, when you are stressed out, you do not function effectively. Everyone has experienced a day when you are so stressed about how much you need to do, that pacing and worrying about how you're going to do it, are all you get done. This happens a lot to people, and it is a gross waste of time. Worrying, no matter how much you do, will not change an outcome. Energy and action are required to get tasks done, so you need to decide what actions to take to reduce or eliminate stressors in your life.

Take a minute, and circle the stressors in your life on any given day. Add your own if they are not listed here:

Friends	Coaches	_____
Boss	Teachers	_____
Health	Customers	_____
Spouse	Students	_____
Money	Employees	_____

You may have identified several of the items as stressors in your life. Multiple stressors will bind up your energy and concentration, rendering them useless in aiding you in your daily routine and preventing you from reaching your goals. It is imperative that you first learn to recognize them, then reduce and eliminate them from your life each day. It may seem too simple when I say this, but it is a fact. "Stress cannot exist if you do not accept it into your brain." You can control your stress by understanding the different roles that you play throughout a day.

Take a minute to identify and circle from this partial list the roles that you may play in a typical day:

Friend	Employee	_____
Parent	Teammate	_____
Accountant	Counselor	_____
Spouse	Self	_____
Employer	Student	_____

If you compare your selections from each of the lists above, you may note that many of them are the same from each list; these are your stressors. The way to reduce stressors is to understand the role that you are playing in any given situation. The point of this test is to recognize your role, accept it, and maximize your potential in that role in an effort to reach your goal.

For example, Let's examine the differences between being your own boss at home and being an employee at your workplace. At home, you are the one in charge of the rules and whether or not they are followed. If they are working well for you, you can choose to leave them intact; however, if there is friction or unbalance in any way, you have the option to incorporate changes that will allow a smoother running home that will enhance your comfort and performance there. At work, however, you are an employee; you have a supervisor and/or manager whose responsibility is to tell you what to do. If you struggle to be the "boss" in the workplace, instead of following your role as an employee, you will be adding stress to your life daily by trying to control matters in which you have no control. However, if you understand that for eight hours a day you are in the role of employee, which means you do your job as directed to the best of your ability, you will eliminate much stress because you are directing your energy to the role you play, and not wasting time and energy trying to control what you can't.

Let's look at another example of reducing stress by understanding the role that you play. Let's pretend you are a teenager, and you are in charge of your younger brother for the evening while your parents are out of town. Now you are assuming the role of parent. It is Friday night; the high school football team is playing, and you want to go to the field, meet your friends, and watch the game. You have a couple of options here. You can allow yourself to be frustrated and stressed, as you envision yourself being stuck at home while your friends are having fun at the game, or you can accept your parental role and take your brother to the game with you. Your brother can meet with his friends and you with yours, as the two of you agree to meet at a designated spot after the game. While this may not be the most desirable situation, you are able to accomplish your goal as well as meet the responsibility of the parent role.

Processing and understanding the various roles that you play in your life and adapting to these roles and the situations that they create will help you reduce and eliminate stress from your life.

It is very important to give thought each and every day to the different roles you are in and will be that day. The best way to understand them is to learn to recognize and become immediately aware of the first signs of the onset of stress. At this point, you need to step back, take a deep breath, "GET-IT Together," and ask yourself what is stressing you and identify what role you are in at the time. This will help you make the best decision for the situation, Remember, control what you can control, and do not try to control what you cannot control.

A great way to reduce stress is by using what I call "natural highs." Natural highs are actions, events, and thoughts that make you feel good. The real benefit of natural highs is that they have no bad side effects like un-natural highs, such as alcohol and drugs.

A natural high will reduce a stressor instantly in your life. I have included a list of natural highs that you can add to your own preferences. I am sure there is literally no end to natural highs, as each individual will have his own.

<u>Natural highs:</u>

Laughing
Watching a stream flow
Getting fit
Being appreciated
Making someone laugh
Puppies wrestling
Enthusiastic people
Hiking
Liking yourself
Children
Running
Smiling
Reading a book
Holding hands

A warm smile
Success stories
Dew on a spider web
Fixing something
A new car
Staring at the stars
Walking on the beach
Snowfall
Watching the sunset
Eating at a nice restaurant
Golfing
Being noticed for your efforts
Helping others
Dancing

<u>Add your own below</u>:

The next time that you are stressed for whatever reason, step back, GET-IT Together, and think of a natural high. You will feel better instantly. The best investment that you will ever make is an investment in your health. Using natural highs to reduce stress is truly an investment in your greatest asset, YOU.

Toolbox takeaway:

Processing and understanding the various roles that you are playing in your life and adapting to these roles and the situations that they create will help reduce and eliminate stress from your life.

Below, list how you can use the tools we have discussed to this point to reduce stress in your life.

_____

_____

_____

_____

_____

_____

It's Great to Be You!

PRODUCTIVITY

"Being productive is looking at today and seeing tomorrow."

D. Faulkner

PRODUCTIVITY

Your productivity is directly related to your income, and it has nothing to do with how much money you make. I would like you to read the following, and then repeat it out loud to yourself.

It takes thirty days to develop or break a habit. If, for the next thirty days, you say the following out loud to yourself and remember to do these things throughout the day, in one month, it is a way of life for you.

I am my greatest asset, and it is great to be me!
Today I will…

⇒ Be productive
⇒ Make good choices
⇒ Pursue my goals

The income I am talking about is the incoming information (attitudes) that you allow into your brain to be processed and then sent back out to the world through your mouth.

When winners, leaders, champions, and warriors are focused on the positive outcomes of their efforts, they do not allow the distractions of negative energies into their brain. Companies all across this country spend millions of dollars on systems that will produce their widgets more efficiently; however, many still have not figured out that they need to invest resources into their greatest asset, the employee. Training in many of the life skills necessary to function normally on a day-to-day basis is needed. Some of these skills include problem solving, stress management, conflict resolution, decision-making processes, and communication. After spending millions on systems, the company still has employees who are coming to work every day with issues from home with which they are unable to deal. This translates into low productivity levels through stress and lack of focus. As stated in the stress chapter, it is very difficult, if not impossible, to function at peak performance when you are stressed by one or more stressors that you do not know how to, nor have the skills to deal with effectively.

A wise investment for any company is to invest in leadership training for its employees. More appropriately, it should be called "life skills" training. Investing in an employee's ability to make good decisions, deal with stress, communicate better, avoid conflict, and become the "I" in team will have a great return on investment towards a company's long-term success goals.

To maximize your productivity potential, you must enjoy what you do and, just as important, feel like your efforts have value and are appreciated. It has been said that in this next decade, there are going to be more jobs available than there are people to fill them. This makes sense with the "baby boomers" retiring.

Armed with that information, it seems to me that the companies that train their employees, give them the life skills that they need, and treat them like they have a value and are appreciated will be successful. Those that do not do this will be out of business because there will not be skilled people available to employ to produce their widgets or provide the services. It will be an "employees' market."

As a company, or individual for that matter, you can be happy with where you are, but you should never be satisfied. You may have everything you ever wanted right now. You can be happy about that, but you should always have a plan for next week, month, year, or decade. Life is in perpetual motion, and whether or not you notice, situations are constantly changing.

Here is a great example of how you should always have a plan even when things seem to be going great. I have a friend, who recently retired from his job as a plant manager for a worldwide manufacturing corporation. He told me this story. Prior to his last job, he was a manager for a company that made analog clocks for the automobile industry. His company had contracts with the "big three" auto makers in the United States. They were very successful and "satisfied" with the large sales volume that they were generating annually out of the plant where he was located. In a matter of twelve months, this successful plant had to close its doors due to lack of sales. What caused this?

Well, it was that year that almost all car companies stopped putting clocks in their vehicles because this function was now being performed by radios and stereo systems that were now digital and had the time function built right into the radio system.

This particular company made clocks, not radios. This may have been a case of being "satisfied" or complacent with today's successes and not looking forward with a vision or plan for the next five years and beyond.

As the "I" in team, your productivity is directly related to your income, and it has nothing to do with how much money you make. It has to do with taking the steps and using the tools necessary for living the life you deserve. It is having the attitude that you are your greatest asset, and it is up to you to create your world.

It is my hope that you live longer than you are employed for the company for which you work. I hope you have a long and happy retirement. Basically, you do not work for company XYZ; you work for YOU. The company gets the great benefit from your productivity, and you get the satisfaction of giving your best every day, setting a high standard of excellence in all you do. This is the difference between going home at the end of a day and being "dog tired" or "good tired." When you go home and are dog tired, you have worked for the wrong reasons. You're not fulfilled, and your productivity has suffered due to the wrong income (attitudes) you have allowed in your day, and you dread going back tomorrow. When you go home good tired, you know you have given your best, earned your keep, and have created the right income (attitudes), allowing you to maximize your productivity. You look forward to going back tomorrow and making a positive contribution. You are the "I" in team, and it's great to be you!

It's Great to Be You!

Toolbox takeaway:

When we become complacent and are satisfied with where we are or what we've done, you can bet someone else will come along and pick up where we slacked off.

Below, list how you provide income (positive attitude) in your life/job and who is affected by it.

_____

_____

_____

_____

_____

_____

_____

_____

_____

_____

Productivity

It's Great to Be You!

DECISION-MAKING PROCESS

"What you do speaks so loud that I cannot hear what you say."

R.W. Emerson

DECISION-MAKING

This is one of the most important tools that you can possess. Good decision-making is important in your ability to solve problems, set goals, develop strategies, and control your day as the "I" in team.

During presentations to companies throughout the country, I frequently ask the audience participants if they believe that they are good decision makers? I will usually get about twenty-five percent at most who believe that they make good decisions. When I ask the others why they believe they do not make good decisions, I get a "deer in the headlights" look followed by a response such as, "I don't know!" This response indicates to me that these people do not understand the "I" in team concept, and they probably are like the pinball that I mentioned in the beginning, being bounced around and having no particular direction in their life. It is hard to be where you want to be in life if you do not take control of the decisions in your life.

As the "I" in team, it is important to have a focus every day. In my life, I use the following as my guide for every day decision-making:

Today I will…
⇒ Be productive
⇒ Make good choices
⇒ Pursue my goals

When you do this, it makes decision-making much easier. As an example, when you are preparing to perform a task you can go quickly through a mental checklist asking yourself, "Is it productive, is it a good choice, and is it getting me closer to my goals?" If it is not going to pass these tests, it is probably not something that you want to invest yourself in.

Once again, we are back at the focus between "cost" and "gain" in all your decisions. The only way that you can truly make decisions that are going to benefit you now and in the future is to know where you are going, and to know where you are going requires that you have goals and a plan as to how you are going to get there.

A lot of people do not like to make decisions because they must then become accountable for the results. While that scares some, it excites those who understand that they are the "I" in team because it puts them in control of the outcome. It allows them to create their own reality.

How do you become a better decision maker? Well, it starts with the four questions that I have posed to you throughout this book.

⇒ Who am I?
⇒ Where am I going?
⇒ What do I want?
⇒ How do I plan to get it?

If you can answer these questions, you have a foundation from which you can base your decisions.

<u>Who are you?</u> This question hits right to your core. Basically, do you like yourself; do you feel comfortable in your skin; are you confident?

<u>Where are you going?</u> This question is asking you to look into yourself and find your "personal roadmap." Which direction are you taking your life?

<u>What do you want?</u> Goals, goals, goals! You must a have a goal for yourself every day! You need to have an idea of what you want to accomplish and where you want to be on purpose.

<u>How are you going to get it?</u> Strategy. What is your plan to get there? Remember, you must factor in the costs of your plan.

When you have developed your answers to these questions, you are armed with the "reasons" to make the right decisions for yourself based on your commitment to YOU, the "I" in team.

I believe taking control of your life and making good decisions are the keys to your personal and professional growth and success. Several years ago, I had a speaking engagement in Milwaukee, WI. I brought my family along, as we planned to go to a Milwaukee Brewers baseball game the next day and make a weekend trip of it.

As we were sitting at a stoplight, an ambulance came speeding through the intersection with its lights flashing and sirens blaring. My son, sitting in the passenger seat, said something under his breath, and with the radio playing, I really could not hear what he said. I turned the radio down and asked him what he just said. His response, coming from a seventeen year old, amazed me. He said, "Somebody's life just changed forever and probably not by his choice." WOW! The person's life in the ambulance probably did change that day. I know of another person's life that changed that day also. It was mine.

Every day, people's lives change as a result of decisions that others make for them. I realized that day, that I need to be able to make good decisions for myself because I am my greatest asset. I am responsible for my happiness and my successes.

If you are not confident in your decision-making abilities, train yourself to ask and answer these four questions - Who am I, where am I going, what do I want, and if I don't have it, how am I going to get it?

Good decision-making is a powerful tool that you can use to maximize your ability to reach your goals and be where you want to be in your life as a result of you, the "I" in team.

Toolbox takeaway:

Taking control of your life and making good decisions are the keys to personal and professional growth and success.

Below, list decisions you make that affect your personal success.

_____

_____

_____

_____

_____

_____

_____

_____

_____

_____

_____

_____

IT DOESN'T MATTER

"Do nothing which is of no use."
                                    M. Musashi

IT DOESN'T MATTER

How many times have you heard someone say, "Oh, that's okay; it doesn't matter," or "Oh, I forgot to get the last items on the list completed for you?" Did you respond with, "That's alright; it doesn't matter in the big picture?"

It does matter! Your life is in perpetual motion; it is constantly changing with each and every second. Everything that you do matters, and everything that you don't do matters. Every action and inaction has a value. As the "I" in team, you need to be constantly aware of what is going on in and around your world. Do you sincerely want to be 100% accountable for your actions? If not, how do you expect to be accountable for the results? Taking control of your life and being accountable for your actions give you the opportunity to be accountable for the results. In other words, being accountable for your actions allows you to be where you want to be in your life and to do it by design (on purpose).

In one-way or another, everyone matters. Every person wants to know that the space she takes up has a value or purpose. Every minute of your waking day should be spent being accountable to you, the "I in team. You should make your personal and professional goals a part of every day. When you are not accountable to yourself and your goals, you are more apt to put tasks off and procrastinate, which pushes your goals farther away.

The length to which people will go to justify why they are

not able to work on their goals is amazing. Over time, I have heard some pretty creative excuses, and most of them are by people who never reach their goals. In this life, you get back what you give. If you give no effort, you get the result of that. Likewise, if you give your time, energy, and passion, you get the result of that. The best part is that you are in charge of this exclusively. Wow! That is exciting!

What you did thirty minutes ago is gone forever; did you waste that time, or use it wisely? Everything matters.

Toolbox takeaway:

Everything that you do matters. Everything that you don't do matters. Every action and inaction has value.

Below, list events, actions, or items in your life that you put energy into which have no value to you and your goals.

_____

_____

_____

_____

_____

It's Great to Be You!

PRIORITIES

"When you know what's right and when you know what's wrong, do what's right!"

R. Saint

PRIORITIES

Setting priorities for yourself and your time is a simple, yet vitally important task. You need to decide what it is that you really want. If you don't have it, you need to develop a plan for how you will get it.

When setting priorities, the necessary tools you will need to make available are energy, time, and commitment. For the next few minutes, let's focus on time.

You may find it helpful to put your budget for time in front of you just as you would your budget for money. That way you can clearly see how much time you have available to work towards your goals on a daily/weekly basis.

Average sleep per day = 7 hours
Average workday = 8 hours
Time spent eating per day = 2 hours
Time getting ready for work per day = 1 hour
Time traveling to and from work per day = 1 hour
Time with family/children per day = 2 hours
Daily errands/appointments per day = 1 hour

This is a hypothetical account of an average day. You could plug in your own personal events and probably come up with similar time commitments on any given day. If you add these, the total comes to twenty-two hours, which leaves you with two hours per day to use for whatever you would like. If you work a forty-hour week Monday through Friday, this will leave you with eight additional hours each on Saturday and Sunday to do with as you please. Most people use these extra weekend hours for errands, appointments, events, family time, traveling, or relaxation.

During the week, you may have only eight hours of available time. This may not seem like much, but if you prioritize, it may be enough to work towards your pursuits and goals. As an example, this book is being written between trainings, on lunch hours, during traveling and at night prior to going to sleep (sometimes falling asleep while typing).

We each have twenty-four hours in a day, so it is not as much about "time management" as about self-management. You are the "I" in team, and what you do with your discretionary time is your choice. You need to take a "time inventory" of your day as you set your goals to discover what time you have available and what time you are willing to allocate towards pursuit of it. Once you decide what time you are able to prioritize for the goal, you will then have a better idea if it is feasible or not. This all figures into the cost of a goal, your true commitment to it, and the expected end result.

VALUE

In the end, it comes down to what value you place on each goal, activity, or task in your life. I find it amazing the amount of people who overlook their health as being a value in their life.

You've heard the saying, "We don't appreciate what we have until we don't have it anymore." This is true and so apparent in many lives today.

Much time is spent on material items and superficial enhancements that don't have lasting value in life. Many hours are spent each week working on physical beauty through makeup, hair, clothes, and colognes, but little time, if any, is spent on building inner beauty with valuables such as love, compassion, integrity, self esteem, faith, and so on.

The paradox is that, the older we get, it does not matter what is done to "enhance it"; our physical beauty deteriorates. However, our inner beauty, the one with lasting value, continues to grow throughout our entire life. Amazingly, these valuable attributes are free to us from the day that we are born; yet many never recognize and take advantage of them. As the "I" in team, you need to understand the value of nurturing these "free" values in your life to maximize your potential.

Another interesting example of the value of our health is that we spend two-thirds of our life either lying in bed sleeping or working on our feet, yet many people will buy the cheapest shoes that they can find, and they will use the same mattress, sometimes, for their entire adult life! The reasoning that I often hear for this is that shoes and mattresses are too expensive. This is where value comes in to the picture. Quality shoes and mattresses should not be looked at as a cost, but, rather, an investment in your health, which should be the priority investment that each and every person should make. I think of it as preventative maintenance.

Since both items are meant to preserve your structure (skeletal and muscular system), which carries you through your life and allows you to be productive, it seems like a "no brainer" that you would want to invest in these areas! Talking with someone with back problems or who has had back surgery should help you realize that a good mattress and a good pair of shoes are not expensive at all. How high on your list of life priorities do you place health?

I believe one of the economic and cultural downfalls in this country began with the sales rack, yes, the clearance racks that promote items at fifty percent off the regular price, two for one, or buy two and get the third free. We began to look only at the price of the products, instead of quality and value. We eventually began to manufacture and sell items that looked as good as the original, but were imitations and not built to the same standard.

About thirty years ago while I was building my own businesses and being a leader in companies for which I have worked, an elderly gentleman said the following to me, and it affected the course of my life, "Son, do you have the time and money to do it right, or the time and money to do it twice?"

When I owned a health club, I chose value first; I made the decision to buy high quality equipment once, rather than "cheaper equipment" several times. My time is valuable, as I am sure yours is, and to do tasks two and three times because you are trying to "cut corners" is not a good investment of time or money, and, therefore, not a good value. Sometimes people will trip over a dime to pick up a penny! Value and service, good and bad, will always sell. Many times you will come to a fork in the road in your life where you have the option of taking "Price Avenue" or Value Boulevard." Which direction are your priorities going to lead for the long-term success of you, the "I" in team?

Toolbox takeaway:

You need to take a "time inventory" of your day as you set your goal, to decide what time you have available and what time you are willing to allocate towards pursuit of it.

Below, list your personal time inventory for a typical week.

_____

_____

_____

_____

_____

FEAR OF FAILURE
(F.O.F. FACTOR)

"Fear is no greater than the power we allow it."

                                                                              D. Faulkner

FEAR OF FAILURE

When striving to reach your goals and become successful on purpose, it is important to consider fear. Fear of failure (F.O.F.) is one of the main obstacles that prevent people from pursuing their dreams and goals. As I have stated in previous chapters, people do not like to fail. In fact, most people are so afraid of failure, it prevents them from ever stepping out to seize their dreams and goals. Many times, our fears are not real, and imagined fears will dictate our actions and take up too much of our time and energy. Due to the fear of failure, many brilliant ideas never come to light because fear causes us to think of "what's wrong" instead of "what's right" in our dreams, ideas, and actions. We focus so much energy thinking of why it will fail, that very little focus is given to why we could be successful if we would just move ahead with our plans. The following is an example of imagined fears.

Imagine that you are on your way home from a long trip, and it begins to rain. You find yourself in the midst of a severe thunderstorm, and it is getting dark. As fate would have it, you make a wrong turn somewhere and find yourself on a dark, dirt road. The rain is pouring down, making it extremely difficult to see the road, which is becoming muddier and softer by the minute.

Imagined fears are already beginning to form as you realize that you have not seen another vehicle in over an hour and you are alone on this dark road. As you stop your vehicle to make a call home on your cell phone, you realize that you have no service.

Fears begin to overtake your senses as you realize that you have no way of communicating with the rest of the world. You try to get back on your way, but the dirt road has now become so soft that the tires only spin as though they are on ice. Your fears are intensifying, and as you look out your windshield, you see a faint light quite a ways up the road, which appears to be a farmhouse.

You're thoroughly frightened now. You do not want to leave your vehicle; you roll the window down and peer ahead only to discover that well before the farmhouse is an old covered bridge. If you decide that you are brave enough to leave your warm, dry car to go to the farmhouse for help, the only path available to you is through the long, dark, and ominous bridge. The wind is howling through the trees as the rain is blowing in sheets across the road, making it almost impossible to see. The old, wooden bridge is creaking and moaning in the storm, and it conjures up all kinds of thoughts and visions from stories and movies of murders and kidnappings. You are really frightened now as your imagined fears confirm that imminent danger lies ahead for you. As you realize that you have no choice but to get out of your car and try to "make it" to the farmhouse, you are terrified because you have spent every second of the last hour working yourself into a fear-filled frenzy.

The reality of the situation is this: you may think that you are scared to walk through the long, dark covered bridge because you have filled yourself with all of this imagined fear. However, if you heard your child or loved one on the other side of the covered bridge, calling out to you for help, you would go through that bridge as fast as you can without any fear at all. In a situation such as that, you would think of "what's right," and your imagined fear would disappear instantly.

Fear is no greater than the power we allow it. If we would think with logic and common sense in most situations in our life, we would realize more successes than failures. While failure comes through fear and denial, success comes through determination and desire.

Anytime you have an idea or are asked to do a job or task that may be outside your comfort zone, try to think of "what's right" and all of the reasons why it "will" work so that you can keep imagined fear out of play. This allows you to move towards your goal with a clear mind and strategy.

Noting that ninety percent of the situations that we fear never happen, consider how much quicker our personal and professional goals could be realized if we would focus on them, instead of our imagined fears.

Without a doubt, the removal or control of imagined fear will yield many brilliant ideas, happenings, and successes in your life.

Toolbox takeaway:

Many brilliant ideas never come to light because fear causes us to think of what's wrong instead of what's right in our dreams, ideas, and actions.

Below, list the fears you have that keep you from maximizing your potential.

_____

_____

_____

_____

_____

_____

_____

_____

_____

_____

_____

It's Great to Be You!

LEADERSHIP

"I am only one, but still I am one. I cannot do everything, but still I can do something. And because I cannot do everything, I will not refuse to do something that I can do."

H. Keller

LEADERSHIP

Leadership is a rather generic word to me. Leadership can come in many different forms from philosophical to psychological to action-based. Leaders are not born; they are made. This supports my position that understanding you are the "I" in team and working to nurture your skills will better assure your chances of being a leader in your life, if that is what you want.

You nurture and sharpen your skills by using the tools discussed in this book to maximize your potential. Some people want to lead others while some want to be in control and just lead themselves towards their particular goals.

Self-leadership is having a goal, creating a vision of that goal, developing a strategy, providing action and energy, and then making a commitment to see that vision come to fruition. Leadership of others is having the ability to inspire others to be their best, many times, beyond their belief.

Leadership is a state of mind; it's a character, a discipline, a focus, and a passion. Leadership is using the "success triangle" on purpose, whether it is self-leadership or leadership of others.

A classic leadership trait is always to be looking ahead and not wasting time looking back. Herb Kelleher, co-founder of Southwest Airlines, is quoted as saying, *"I never look back; really I don't. When people ask me what I did yesterday, I can't answer them. I'm not faking it. I try to remain directed forward. It's convenient to forget about all the mistakes I've made."*

Herb Kelleher is a true leader in the airline industry. When he started his airline, he virtually looked at everything that the industry was doing, and he did just the opposite. Southwest has always focused on its commitment to their employees and providing value for their customers.

Leaders do not waste time bemoaning their mistakes and allowing them to stifle further efforts. They examine them, learn from them, and then move forward, being wiser for the experience and knowledge learned. Holding onto a mistake is like putting a kink in a hose, not letting the positive energy flow freely. In the chapter called "It Doesn't Matter," I told you that what you did thirty minutes ago is gone forever. Did you use the time wisely, or did you waste it? There is no need to hold on to the mistake, let it go.

This is a story of a Zen master and his disciples coming back from a journey to find true enlightenment. As a monk, you were not to think about women, look at women, or touch women. It was thought that women cloud the true minds of men (I am not saying this, so do not shoot the messenger!). As the story goes, the monks were walking along a river's edge when they heard a cry for help. It was coming from the river, which was quite fierce, as the white-capped waves crashed into everything with which they came in contact. Amidst the waves was a woman who was screaming and fighting for her life, as the river was pulling her down stream. As the master monk noticed this, he immediately, without conscious thought, jumped into the raging river to save the life of this terrified woman. He was able to get her to the edge, and he carried her out of the water with her clinging to his body like a lost and scared child. As the master put her down, she hugged and kissed him, while thanking him for saving her life! The master and his disciples went on their way. As they were walking, the master noticed that one monk in particular seemed to be quite upset. He was kicking the dirt and arguing with himself along the way. When they finally reached the gates of the monastery, the master went to the disciple and asked what was wrong. The disciple answered, "You are a hypocrite, Master; you tell us that we cannot look, touch, or think of women, yet you recognize a woman and put her in your arms. She kisses and hugs you before you let her go. I do not understand." The master replied, "I saved the life of another human being, my disciple; then I set her down to be free. You have carried her for ten miles!"

This is what happens when you try to control what you cannot control. You become stressed and angry, and you cannot function properly. Leadership is having the ability to let situations go and move forward. Using the GET-IT concept, you should enhance your "inner skills" through whatever situation you are faced, and then you will move forward and become a better person.

Rather than giving you examples of leaders and what they

have done, I would like to have you decide who the leaders are in your world. What is it about those you select as leaders that sets them apart or makes you want to follow their way of life? This way, you will have a working model to use that is just for you, while striving either to change the way you operate or continue to enhance your skills towards a specific goal in an area of your life. Grab your pen; answer the following questions about leadership.

Who are people in your life whom you would identify as leaders?

What traits do they have that you believe make them leaders?

Which of these traits do you believe that you have working for you?

Which of these traits, not already in place, do you need to develop?

After filling in the answers to these questions, you should have an idea of what you are already doing and what you need to do to maximize your potential and become the leader who you want to be.

Leadership-minded people always expect more from themselves than they do others. Most people are just the opposite, expecting perfection from everyone else; however, when it comes to themselves, it is okay to "renegotiate the standard" to justify why it could not be completed or finished. Leadership-minded people take ownership in ALL of their actions.

As a little help for you, I have included the "personal contract" that I use with my leadership retreats and workshops. One benefit of this contract is that you need to have at least one person (spouse, friend, or family member) sign this contract with you. The contract states your commitment to your new goals and strategies. By doing this, you are not only accountable to you, but also accountable to someone else who has value to you in your life.

Leadership does not blame or make excuses. Leadership is ownership, and as the "I" in team, you must understand that you own your attitude, actions, and results.

Toolbox takeaway:

Leadership is a state of mind, it's a character, a discipline a focus, and a passion.

Leadership

PERSONAL CONTRACT

From this day forward, I, _____, will work on the following areas to maximize my potential and to be my best at everything that I do.

1. _____

2. _____

3. _____

If I do not set a standard of excellence for myself, I accept mediocrity (average) as being good enough for me. <u>No one ever rewards average effort.</u> It is the spirit of being your best that will bring you reward. Upon signing this contract, I will set myself up for success by giving my best ALWAYS and NEVER accepting average effort for my greatest asset, MYSELF.

I sign this contract on this ____day of_____ in the year of _____.

NAME   **WITNESS**

_____   _____

COMMUNICATION

"Communication, or the lack thereof, is the great divide between success and failure."

R. Saint

COMMUNICATION

Have you ever asked a co-worker to do something for you, and he agreed to get it done, but when you returned, it wasn't done to your standards? Maybe you asked your child to clean his room, and later when you examined the room, you gave a look of disgust as you said, "I thought that I asked you to clean your room?" Your child answered, "I did." Well, the fact is that the person you asked to do something for you did exactly what he thought you wanted done, and your child did exactly what he heard you ask him to do. The problem is that you took for granted that he would know what your expectations were.

Had you taken the time to ask your co-worker if it was clear to him what you expected, you would have realized one of two outcomes: your co-worker didn't have a clear understanding of what you had expected, or he did understand and did as you asked. Your child also did what you asked him to do, but, because his concept of cleaning a room differs from yours, he cleaned his room to his own satisfaction. Although cleaning to you may mean dusting the furniture, changing the linens, and putting away all of his clothes, it may not mean the same for him. Had you stated clearly what you expected, "I want you to dust your furniture, change the linens and so on," he would have known what you expected from him and would have been able to carry out the tasks to your specifications.

Communication should be an easily used tool that helps us

deliver a message clearly. However, some people struggle to use it effectively. This is partly because most people believe that everyone thinks just like they do; however, all people process information that they receive differently. Over twenty-three hundred years ago, Hippocrates wrote that people could be categorized into four distinctive groups. Those who have good communication skills understand that listening is an important part of communication. I think it was talk show host Larry King who said, "Nothing I say this day will teach me anything. So if I am going to learn, I must do it by listening." We have one mouth and two ears for a reason!

As the "I" in team, it is important that you be a good listener. In order to reach your goals through good communication skills, there are three areas of communication that you need to focus on to help you GET-IT Together.

First is proxemics or personal space. All of us have been in a situation where we have been trying to work with or talk to someone who insists on standing or sitting too close to us. Because it makes us feel uncomfortable, instead of being able to concentrate on the conversation, we find ourselves concentrating on how uncomfortable we are. Why is this happening? It is because the other person has entered our personal space. Here is how to determine your personal space: Take your arms, hold them out to the side, and turn around in a circle. This is your personal space, and no one has a right to be in that space unless you let or want him there. It does not necessarily mean that the other person is trying to upset you or even be aware that he has. It may simply be that his personal space for himself is different than yours is for you. If the "closeness" makes you uncomfortable, you need to clarify your intent and ask the person to back up because he is too close. He will probably do so. You need to also be aware of the personal space of others. Let's say that you are going for a job interview and you are in the office with the human resource manager. As the interview starts, you lean forward and rest your arms on the desk as you begin talking. You may see the HR manager lean back and pull the interview form back towards herself. This tells you that you are too close and getting into her personal space. Always be aware of others' personal space, as well as your own.

Secondly is kinesics or body language. Studies now say that up to ninety-seven percent of all communication is nonverbal. In observing people as they communicate with you, the nonverbal message may be as strong, if not stronger than what they are verbalizing to you, and sometimes it may be completely the opposite of what they are verbally saying! As the director of Safety and Employee Development for the Midwest packaging company I mentioned earlier, I answered to the Vice President. During a meeting with him one day, I was telling him about an issue that we had that really meant a lot to me and I thought it was important. After a few minutes of talking, I noticed that he began looking at his watch and shuffling a few papers around as he was responding with generic responses. As the corporate trainer who taught communication skills for the company, I recognized at this point that he was no longer listening to me, so I shut down the conversation and left the office. That was nonverbal communication at its best. He was no longer hearing a word that I was saying, so for me to keep talking would have been a useless waste of time for both of us.

Lastly, is (para verbal communication) or how you say what you say. Listening to how people say what they are saying will tell you a lot. This is done through their cadence, tone, and volume. Some people have a tendency to talk too loudly for the situation while others will almost whisper when they talk, making it difficult to understand them. As an example, listen to the tone of a person when he is holding and enjoying a small pet, such as a dog. His tone is similar to one used when talking to a newborn baby. In contrast, listen to the tone when he is scolding or disciplining that dog. Based on the tone of a conversation, you can get a really good sense of the feeling, emotion, or intent someone is trying to project to you.

Many times, as with the GET-IT Together concept, it is the presentation, or more precisely, the communication technique, that one is using to reach his goal that will determine the outcome.

Let's look at it like music, a universal language. Over the years, music has influenced many people in many cultures throughout the world. There are many different styles of music such as rock and roll, country, blues, jazz, folk, heavy metal, classical, and many more types too numerous to mention. The two styles that I will use to make my point are classical and rock and roll. Many people, including the practitioners of each style, would probably say they are on opposite ends of the musical spectrum. However, they may not be as different as they appear. Let's take a look.

First, there is classical music. Many classical musicians are well schooled in their art. They begin playing as a child; many are born into it through family history. When they reach the proper age, they are sent to a private music school to study. Here, they study the history of the music, as well as the instrument that they play. Classical music is usually performed at levels of high social standing. Classical music can usually be seen at music halls, in theaters, or on Broadway. Classical artists are viewed as "good people" who are socially accepted.

Secondly, we have rock and roll musicians. These artists are stereotypically viewed as being high school dropouts with nothing better to do than make a lot of noise, grow their hair long, and cause social disturbance. These artists are portrayed as living lives filled with drugs, alcohol, and wild women. Today, there are those who say rock and roll music is the cause of suicide and even murder among its listeners.

Now, I will compare the two styles and make my point about communication. I have been to rock and roll concerts and seen people screaming at the top of their lungs with excitement as the music being played was giving them a great feeling of happiness.

I have also seen classical performances when people will look at each other, after a great piano piece, and smile because the music gave them a great feeling of happiness.

I have seen people crying at a rock and roll concert, as a ballad being performed reminded them of a personal experience in their lives. By the same token, I have seen classical plays where the music had reached a level during a sad moment, causing people to express their feelings with tears.

The point is that music demands emotion and expression. It does not matter what style it is.

There are only twelve notes on the chromatic scale, and they are available to all styles of music. Wow! Millions of songs from different styles and none sounding exactly alike come from only twelve notes. Therefore, there really aren't great differences in music itself; the difference is in the ***presentation.***

When you are communicating with others, it is of paramount importance that you use the communication tools mentioned earlier to develop the communication technique that you will use to express your intent.

After all, good communication is the exchange of information between parties, where all participants listen to and hear the same message.

Toolbox takeaway:

Communication should be an easily used tool that helps us deliver a message clearly. However, some people struggle to use it effectively.

Below, list your communication strengths and their effectiveness on different people in your life.

_____

_____

_____

_____

_____

_____

_____

_____

_____

_____

_____

INTENT

Intention
Behavior
Perception

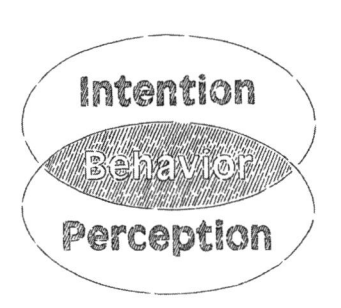

"We are what we repeatedly do, excellence, then, is not an act but a habit."

Aristotle

INTENT

Understanding the three elements of communication presented in the previous chapter will help you understand another's true intentions. People may talk or communicate with you, though their conversation has nothing to do with their intent. Years ago I owned a health club which was located on the main street in the community. This high traffic area was the preferred route of salespeople and others whose main goal was to get businesses to donate to a particular cause. A gentleman walked into my club one day and with a big smile said, "Hello Ray, how are you today?" My response was this, "I am fine, thank you. WHO are you?" I had never met this man before, yet he was calling me by my first name, acting as though we had been friends for years. I assumed that he had asked the business owner next door who owned the health club, so when he came in and saw me behind the counter, the percentage was quite good that I was Ray, the owner. Now, knowing his intent was not pure, I clarified my intent of wanting to know who "my new best friend" was by coming right out and asking him, "who are you?" As it turned out, he was selling products, for which I had no use, so I wished him success, and he went on his way to meet his next new, best friend.

Clarifying your intent and being aware of what is the true intent of others will benefit you greatly in your life. It removes the gray area from communication.

In the 1980's, I was the safety and security operations leader at an international corporation. We had six thousand employees at our corporate headquarters location. Being responsible for the day-to-day safety operations for my department of twenty-five employees meant that we had to have good communication with no gray areas for mistakes.

The best way to do this was to avoid communication errors by clarifying my intent when giving directives. If I asked the third shift leader to get the speed bumps down in the parking lot, I gave him simple and concise instructions as to where, how many, the deadline and so on. I then asked if he understood me, and he replied O.K. I would be on my way. WRONG! This is where gray area mistakes occur.

After I asked if he understood me, I then said to him, "Because this is a very important function for the safety of our employees and it is important that it be done correctly, would you please repeat to me what I would like you to do?" If he responded with a clear understanding, then I knew it would get done correctly. If he did not, we would go over the process again until we both were satisfied.

I just used the "three arts of a warrior" to communicate my message. To clarify this for you, a "warrior" is a loving, nurturing human being who has a genuine respect for life. A warrior is the opposite of a "monster" who is a person who goes around trying to hurt others or take things that do not belong to him. The first art of the warrior is intention; the second art is perception, and the third art is behavior. Intention is one's goal; perception is the emotion/

energy that arises, and behavior is the action that springs from the previous two.

Using the speed bump scenario, when I clarify my intent (goal) of getting the speed bumps in place, the shift leader I was speaking to will get the perception (emotion/energy) from my directive that this is an important function that must be done correctly. That perception will dictate his behavior (action), and the task will get done. Why? People do not want to fail, and when they are given the proper expectations and tools, they will produce.

Intention + Perception = Behavior

Not only do you need to clarify your intention when communicating so that the task is done correctly, it is just as important that the employee understands his value in carrying out the assignment. As I have stated earlier, people do not want to fail or be disciplined for something that they believed they did correctly.

There are four primary intentions of people: *Power, pleasure, avoidance of responsibility, love and respect.* Each of these intentions will differ from individual to individual as far as what each means; however, these are the four primary intentions of which you should be aware when communicating with others in determining their true goal.

When you master these communication skills, you allow the "I" in team in each individual to be maximized, which will create a strong team, organization, or family.

Toolbox takeaway:

Clarifying your intent and being aware of the true intent of others will benefit you greatly in your life.

List your goals and confirm their intent.

_____

_____

_____

_____

_____

_____

_____

_____

_____

It's Great to Be You!

5 SYSTEMS OF THE BODY

"A man too busy to care for his health, is like a mechanic too busy to care for his tools."

French Proverb

5 SYSTEMS OF THE BODY

The human body is amazing! The systems of the body work together like a fine machine to allow you to function in many different capacities and environments throughout your life. They protect and serve you even though you often abuse them on a regular basis. Let's look at some of the ways that you might abuse your systems.

With the fast moving pace of today's society and lifestyles, you often don't have the time or you don't take the time to eat regularly and fuel your body as you should. When you do take time to eat, it is often on the run, and your body isn't allowed to slow down and relax, which in turn undermines healthy digestion. In turn, this tends to make you eat more and to choose the wrong foods, which eventually make you susceptible to disease.

Many years ago when I was a young man training in the martial arts, I attended a seminar on inner power and the cultivation of your inner energies. One section of this workshop was dedicated to food and nutrition. While there was a lot of useful information presented, the one statement that I remember most was what one master of inner power shared with us as we were headed for lunch. He said, " Be sure to eat slowly, and taste your food because you are not just eating food. You are treating your body with a gift; you are rewarding your body for taking care of you."

Substance abuse is another way that you might abuse your systems. Substance abuse not only weakens your mind, leaving you open to making irrational and wrong choices which may adversely affect your body, but also causes you to eat at times when you really are not hungry and when your body is not requiring fuel. Along with other contributors, substance abuse may cause you to eat more than you utilize daily, leaving you de-conditioned. Substance abuse over an extended period of time will eventually affect all of your body's systems.

Even with the situations I've mentioned above, the body is a unique machine with many checkpoints that help it adapt and overcome your constant abuse until the day that, it adapts to as much as it can and begins to shut down, usually in the form of illness.

As the "I" in team, it is important that you are aware of the five main systems and their functions that give us the opportunity to reach our goals. Those systems are the following:

Nervous system
Circulatory system
Musculature system
Skeletal system
Respiratory system

Nervous System

Long-term decision-making concerning your health requires both a healthy mind and a healthy body. It is difficult, if not impossible, to make healthy decisions if you are living in a cloud of drugs, alcohol, stress, anger, sadness, jealousy, and greed. These conditions and emotions, of which you can and should have control, are like a hose with a kink in it, constantly restricting its flow. In this case, instead of water, it is the flow of energy, ideas, and actions that are being inhibited and suppressed in your daily life and decision-making. The brain is a muscle, and it needs to be exercised continually. Since the mind harbors what the body manifests, it makes sense that nurturing and growing the mind's capacity will benefit your body as well. Many of the functions of the central nervous system are taken care of for you without conscious thought, which frees you to focus on the elements that you can control, such as using your brain and giving the body the proper nutrition it needs to function at maximum capacity. You need to do this on purpose.

Circulatory System

This is the system that, simply put, involves the blood and heart. Blood travels through our body, which is pumped by the heart, picking up vital minerals and nutrients along the way. You have a lot of input and decision about the health of this system.

You can exercise to strengthen your heart "muscle," and you can monitor your nutrition and take care of your blood to avoid diabetes and other illnesses that affect your health. You must consider your body as the vessel that carries and sustains your life. You can and should do everything possible to balance and maximize your body's potential.

Musculature System

The system of muscles performs an important function. Muscles, along with ligaments and tendons, keep our skeletal system erect and intact. Without these, our bones would crumble to the ground. After the age of thirty-five, we will lose 1 ½ percent of our muscle mass every year unless we do something to maintain it, such as moving, working, and exercising. The reason the elderly so often fall and break their hips or legs is because they have little muscle mass to support their structure. It is important that you stretch every day because your muscles are "continuous tension members," which means they are constantly pulling inward and you need to stretch them to keep them working at maximum capacity. Often when one "pulls" a muscle it is because it was not stretched and prepared to handle the load put on it. Notice how many elderly people walk - they take short, little scooting steps, not because they want to, but because it is all that they can do. Their hamstring muscles no longer have the elasticity they once had, and they tighten up and pull in along with the tendons and ligaments. Your body will eventually wear out, just like the moving parts of a car do. Your goal should be to take care of and maintain your body so that it will give you the most years of both the highest and maximum performance as possible.

Skeletal System

Bones are living tissue. They support the "framework" that supports your other systems. Keep your structure strong. One of the easiest steps that you can do to keep your bones healthy is to have the right diet. A diet rich in the important bone nutrients is vital for supporting optimal bone function. Calcium, vitamin D, vitamin K_1, magnesium, zinc, and protein are considered the key bone nutrients. Another key step in keeping your bones healthy is to limit alcohol, coffee, and other caffeinated drinks daily. Staying active is also important. Try to include some weight bearing activities every day.

Respiratory System

We talked about this in an earlier chapter. As with the other systems, you can nurture and care for this system by exercising to strengthen your lungs as well as by getting proper nutrition. This system processes and maximizes the use of oxygen to support the other systems. As I said earlier, if you close your mouth and pinch your nose, in about three minutes, you will recognize the value of the respiratory system. (Please take my word for it, and do not try it!)

A common thread in these major systems is nutrition and exercise. I have read that almost all ailments of the organs and structures of the body can be traced back to a lack of proper nutrition and lack of exercise. The real goal in all of life is to try to find a balance. A balance of your five body systems, a balance between work and play, a balance between quiet time and hectic pace are all vital. This is not always easy to do; however, if you learn to become continually aware of and focus on the importance of balancing your life, you should be able to maximize your potential as the "I" in team.

As I've stated before, life is simple; it's just not easy. These five body systems are very powerful, and they are what makes us better than machines. A five horsepower machine can operate at its level; however, if you try to push it beyond the capabilities built into it, it will develop problems or even break down completely.

Your body, on the other hand, which operates at a particular level, can be built up, strengthened, and maintained, and over time it can be empowered to operate at a higher level if you are willing to work with it.

What I want to impress upon you is that these systems have been given to you to nurture, develop, and maintain them at their healthiest state, to operate to your advantage in your life. We don't have to wake up every morning and wonder how our nervous system is functioning today. We do not need to wonder because our nervous system, as well as the remaining four major systems of our body, automatically regulates themselves. But it is our responsibility to see to it that they are given the important nutrients, exercise, and rest in proper balance in order to assure them the ability to regulate themselves and operate at their highest and healthiest state. I believe as the "I" in team, you should do tasks because you want to and not because you have to. Do not wait until you have to constantly check your blood sugars every day. Control what you take into you body now in order to ward off diabetes and other life altering and threatening illnesses before they strike, impairing your body's ability to function properly. You should always make it a priority to know what is going on with your body and your systems. Although many actions in life are not in your control, you are in control of what you choose to give your attention, and you should make your health a top priority before it becomes a "have to" priority.

It is interesting that some people never have time to focus on getting or staying healthy, but when they "have to" focus on their health due to disease or sickness, they can always make time. Wow! Heavy stuff!

Toolbox takeaway:

Although many things in life are not in your control, you are in control of what you choose to give your attention, and you should make your health a top priority before it becomes a "have to" priority.

Below, list your commitments to your mind and body maintenance and development.

_____

_____

_____

_____

_____

_____

5 Systems of the Body

It's Great to Be You!

INSPIRATION

"Motivation is not something that you give to someone. Inspiration is what you give to people so that they can motivate themselves towards achieving personal and professional success."

R. Saint

INSPIRATION

Today we live in a world where practically any dream can become reality. More than any other time in history, we have the tools necessary at our fingertips to pursue our dreams, and we have opportunity to make these dreams come true. While we need people with brilliant ideas, even more importantly, we need leaders who are capable of taking the dreams and making them a reality. The difference between a dreamer and a leader is action. While one person may dream, another will take action necessary to make his dreams come true. What makes a person want to be good, help others, or maximize his potential? What encourages a leader to put dreams into action? I believe it is inspiration.

Anyone can be motivated, but the spark that ignites the motivation into action is inspiration, and it varies in each individual. In the Success Triangle that we spoke about earlier, we talked about the three elements of Motive, Desire, and Opportunity. It is in desire where I believe one finds his passion and inspiration.

In my twenty-six years of teaching and training in the martial arts disciplines of Tae Kwon Do and Hap Ki Do, I have always been a self-motivated person with a tremendous passion for martial arts. No matter what you do for a living, I believe that there will always be peaks and valleys along your journey. When you are on a peak, everything seems to click into place. Your skills are very sharp, and you are excited about every movement. When you are in a valley, you may feel complacent and not on top of your game. No matter what your vocation, I am confident that you have experienced peaks and valleys in your life.

I believe that you need to continually remind yourself of what motivates you to do what you do. It is just as vital to stay plugged into positive reinforcement, whether it is a person, seminar, or book to re-inspire you or to keep you inspired.

I have always told my students that if you want to have a hero, strive to become a person of motivation and desire, so uniquely inspirational that you can be your own hero. While I still believe this is good advice, it was just about five years ago that I was fortunate enough to have crossed paths with a young man who since has become my hero. This young man walked into the Tae Kwon Do school one day and changed me forever. Over the years, I have instructed students with impediments ranging from cerebral palsy to deafness. Each was an inspiration and are true leaders in their lives. However, after getting to know Dusty and learning about the obstacles that he overcame in his short life, I began to realize that, as long as you can inhale and exhale, it is almost impossible to have a bad day. Here is his story.

I first met Dusty at a belt testing in one of my satellite schools. I attend all belt tests at each school, not only to see the students, but also to ensure that the techniques are remaining pure and not getting watered down. Dusty walked in with a bit of a hitch in his step, which caused him to lean to one side of his body. I recall our first meeting to this day; however, what stuck out to me more than his physical abnormality, was his infectious attitude. Prior to the testing, the students warm up on their own and talk amongst each other, comparing notes or quizzing one another about the test as they prepare to go to the next belt level. Although he looked serious and ready to do his best, Dusty always had a positive attitude and was always willing to help others.

Dusty, born with a hole in his heart and a bad valve, had his first open-heart surgery when he was five days old. At one year old, he had another open-heart surgery, and the same evening after the surgery, his lung collapsed. At this time, the doctors diagnosed him with severe scoliosis of the spine. When Dusty was nine years old, he had surgery to fuse vertebrae, at which time the doctors attached two stainless steel rods to his spine. In June of 2008, Dusty had a third open heart surgery to replace the valve in his heart with a pig valve.

I did not tell you about Dusty so that you will feel sorry for him, I mentioned him because he is an inspiration to me (and everyone whom he meets) as a leader, and he is definitely the "I" in team. Dusty remains one of the hardest working students I have seen in my years as an instructor, every day maximizing his potential and never wasting a minute. What inspires me the most about Dusty is his effort. He truly set a standard of excellence for himself and never accepted anything less. That is being "extra" ordinary and successful on purpose. With two steel rods in his back, Dusty had every "excuse" to not even train in the martial arts because of his handicap. But he chose not to use the "poor-poor me" option; instead, he took the high road of "I can be my best at whatever I do." Dusty became an assistant instructor and leader of others at the Tae Kwon Do school and is now attending college to pursue his passions.

Whenever I feel tired or I struggle to reach a peak in my life, I think of Dusty and what he has accomplished in his life, against all odds, and it quickly enables me to regain solid footing and resume my climb. The story of Dusty is truly an inspiration for me.

I am sure that you have a story in your life that is extraordinary and inspirational. It does not matter what it is about or from where it came. What matters is that it sparks your motivation so that you can maximize your true potential.

Now go out there and find it!

It's Great to Be You!

<u>Toolbox takeaway</u>:

You need to continually remind yourself of what motivates you to do what you do.

Below, list inspirations in your life and how you use them.

_____

_____

_____

_____

_____

_____

_____

_____

_____

_____

_____

Inspiration

It's Great to Be You!

WHAT'S RIGHT?

"First, a person told me there was a 30% chance of rain. A second person told me that there was a 70% chance of sunshine. I believe the second person."

R. Saint

WHAT'S RIGHT?

As a whole, people normally ask, "What's wrong?" We tend to look at what's wrong in our life and what is going wrong in our day, overlooking the events and happenings that are running smoothly. We skim right past the positives in our life that are going right, never rewarding them. To find what's right in your life, the first action to take is change the color of window through which you are viewing life. This will change your outlook on life, and it will move you forward with positive results. As an example, let's use a block of large, beautiful, and well-kept homes, and in the middle of the block sits a quaint, little cottage that hasn't been updated since the mid-forties. How would you view the homes on that block? Would you say, "Look at those beautiful homes on that block," or would you say, "Look at the outdated house sitting there in the middle of those beautiful homes?" Let's use the beautiful well-kept homes as positive thoughts and actions in your day, and the outdated cottage represents the negative thoughts and actions in your day.

The majority of people will focus on the outdated house, or negative attitude, when they should look at the large beautiful homes and then view the small cottage in the condition that is has the potential to become. A few years ago when I was mowing the grass at the golf driving range that I owned, I had just finished mowing ten acres of grass on the range and drove my lawn mower out to the frontage grass by the highway to mow it last. As I was mowing, I looked back towards the ten beautiful acres of fresh mown grass. There, sticking up in front of the tee line just before the freshly mowed fairway of grass was a tall weed. I actually stopped the mower, stared at the weed, and chuckled to myself as I thought, most people would look at this scene and focus on the weed, totally missing the beautifully groomed ten acres of lawn. Too often, we do this in our lives, and it prevents us from reaching our goals and being successful. We tend to focus on the negative events that make up about five percent of our day and ignore the positive actions, which make up ninety-five percent of the day. Do you recognize the weeds in your life, the roadblocks that seem so prominent that you miss all the good by focusing your attention on the ugly? Where you place your focus is where you will expend your energy, and that will dictate the outcome or action. On the average, most of our days are filled with positive actions, such as greeting a friend, hugging your child, working with co-workers to solve issues and challenges, or simply being nice and showing common courtesies to those around you. When you focus on the negative forces around you, they infiltrate your thoughts and take your mind from the positives, and, eventually, they erode your attitude.

Think about what you see on television or read in the newspapers. Much of it is negative, and if you hear it enough, you become desensitized. Sitting in a cafeteria or in a meeting, you hear people talk about what they have read in the newspapers or heard on the radio. You can see how the negative energy spreads from the affected person and affects everyone in the room. Do not be fooled by thinking that this does not matter (remember, everything matters) because it will erode your attitude and eventually affect your actions/outcomes if you are not careful. We tend to become products of our environment, so it is important not to allow yourself to be in these negative environments for too long.

Begin each day looking at what is going right instead of what's going wrong. Reinforce these things by saying them out loud to yourself. Throughout the day, when you hear people talking about what's wrong at work, in the grocery store, at bowling league or anywhere, remind yourself of something that is right in your day.

For every action, there is an equal and opposite reaction (nature's law), so in order to continue to grow in a positive attitude, you need to think of two or more positives because the first "positive" cancels the "what's wrong" and the second "positive" gets your attitude growing in the right direction.

Before you go to bed each night, I suggest putting a note pad beside your bed, to jot down all of the positive actions that you performed throughout the day. Thanking someone for dinner, saying hello to an acquaintance, to helping a co-worker. You will be surprised at the amount of positive acts that you perform in a single day! Winners, leaders, champions, and warriors always take the time to recognize the positive. What better way to go to sleep and get a good night's rest, than to fall asleep with positive thoughts of what you, the "I" in team, did to make the world a better place. When you wake up, you can look at the list as a way to remind yourself of what is right, as you take advantage of the opportunity to get out there and win another day!

Toolbox takeaway:

When you focus on the negative forces around you, they infiltrate your thoughts, take your mind from the positives, and, eventually, erode your attitude. Stay positive!

Below, list what's right in your life.

_____

_____

_____

_____

_____

_____

_____

_____

_____

_____

_____

It's Great to Be You!

LIFESTYLE CHANGE

"Give us the tools, and we will finish the job."

W. Churchill

LIFESTYLE CHANGE

Well, you've come to the end of the book. You have learned about the tools for becoming successful on purpose. You may have agreed with many of the statements throughout the book, and you may have disagreed with some as well. Either way, hopefully you have made some life-changing decisions and chosen the tools that will work for you at any given time in your journey towards reaching your goals on purpose, whatever they may be.

What now? I have a suggestion: DO IT!

Will it be easy, probably not? Can it be done? Of course, it can. What then is the secret that helps some people become leaders, who are successful and happy when others seem to never get anywhere? I hope by this point in the book that you realize that there is no secret; instead, it is a combination of the success triangle and the aforementioned tools. Most importantly, it is the realization that you are the "I" in team, and it is up to YOU.

For most people, there is one more key action to this process, and that is a "lifestyle change." Whether it is to be more positive, lose weight, become self-employed, or pursue your dream, it will require a lifestyle change. You must make a continued commitment to living differently from now on.

If you want to become healthier and you have never worked out regularly, you will have to commit yourself to the fact that you are going to begin working out and continue to perform this action for the rest of your life.

If you want to follow your dream of being self-employed, you may have to give up city league softball or Wednesday night bowling for as long as necessary to commit the time to your new venture.

If you want to change your attitude and become a more positive person, you may have to start reading books with positive influence or stop hanging out in the lunchroom at work where all of the distracting and negative gossip is taking place.

The key to a lifestyle change is to have a plan built into your strategy for when your confidence is weak. I can almost guarantee you will have set backs in attitude because of the negative forces around you. Also, negatives are as much a part of life as positives. We must have both of them. You can buy a $250,000 Rolls Royce, and if you take either the positive or negative battery cable off of the battery, the vehicle will not start. It takes both positive and negative energies to create the "life" or energy needed to maximize potentials.

Habits are formed by building links between brain cells. The more you do something repeatedly, the stronger the links become. When you have a weak day or set back in your attitude, the first thought you will have is to resort to the "old way" of acting because it is to what you are accustomed, and it is easier. What are you going to do to pull yourself out of this? Call a friend whom you can trust to help reinforce your commitments; go for a brisk walk alone, or look in the mirror and ask that million-dollar question, "How bad do I really want what I say I want?"

Whatever tool you need to have in place for the weak moments must be built into your strategy before you begin. I suggest that you keep this book or the pocket guide handy during these times. Sir Winston Churchill said something to this effect, "Champions and leaders do not need to be told what to do, just reminded every once in a while." All of us, no matter how strong we think we are, need consistent reminders of why we are doing what we are doing so that we stay the course.

Hopefully, I have shared with you practical applications of some of the necessary tools for becoming successful on purpose in your life. I hope that you have found value in the time that you have invested in reading this book.

As the "I" in team, you should now understand without a doubt that your commitment to you is ultimately the best way to reach your potential, and, quite frankly, you shouldn't want it any other way.

<u>Toolbox takeaway</u>:

The key to a lifestyle change is to have a plan built into your strategy for the times when your confidence is weak.

It's great to be you!

Thoughts, contemplations, successes, positives

Request Ray Saint LIVE

If you coordinate your organizations live events and would like to request Ray as a speaker, simply go to our website for details and availability.

www.raysaint.com

ALSO AVAILABLE AS AN AUDIO BOOK ON CD

Its Great To Be You is also available on audio compact disc. It is read by the author. A great travel companion! This can be purchased by going to our website and ordering online.

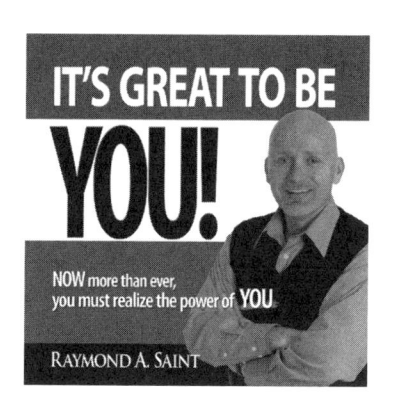

www.raysaint.com

Give the Gift of

"It's Great to Be You!"

To your children, friends
and colleagues!

Visit www.raysaint.com for:

⇒ Quantity pricing

⇒ Speaking availability

⇒ Information and products